Dear Liz,

Simple Strides Toward Positive Change:
Lessons from Life Coaching

all my best!

Susan

Simple Strides Toward Positive Change: Lessons from Life Coaching

Susan Korwin

Project editor: Sheila Buff
Book design: Tony Meisel
Cover design: Devin Korwin
Cover photo: Mark Weiss
Back cover photo: Alan Barry

Library of Congress Cataloging-in-Publication Data is available on request.

ISBN: 978-0-9848838-0-6

Printed in the United States

Contents

Acknowledgements

I want to acknowledge and thank all the many people over the past years who have taken the time to ask me my opinion. This set off the chain reaction of my Facebook fan page, my Life Coach certification, and my ultimate dream . . . the culmination which is this book. I may be an encouragement to you, but your encouragement of me is something I will carry in my heart always. I also want to thank my editor, Sheila Buff, for her dedication and hard work in helping me put into chapter form all my short messages of inspiration. Her knowledge of every aspect of publishing a book was invaluable to me. My love and thanks to Devin Korwin for designing the book cover. My husband, Robert, has taught me more than he can ever realize about life, love and what a soul mate really is.

Why I Wrote this Book

The thoughts that are included in this book can and should be likened to a donation dropped into a secret place in your heart. Maybe one day, in your hour of need, you will remember this gift and withdraw its contents. This is my wish for all of you.

For many years, people, including total strangers, sought my advice on subjects ranging from style to relationships to exercise and personal wellness. I was always quick to help, whether standing on line at the grocery store or while comforting a friend in a dilemma. I truly believe we all have unique talents that should be shared with others. Once my three sons were older, I decided that all the advice I was giving out would make for a great career choice. I worked as a personal shopper, and found that most of my clients regularly criticized their appearance, calling themselves fat and ugly. That always amazed me, because there was no basis for it in reality. It was then that I knew that happiness and a fulfilling life weren't just about the outside. The inside is what needs to be solid if the foundation is to be stable.

I decided to become a Life Coach after realizing the great need for gentle guidance through life's obstacles. The training program through the prestigious Life Coach Institute was a difficult course of reading books, listening to CDs and finally being tested to gain certification. Taking the course taught me a lot and helped me adjust my thinking and reactions. Just as a coach runs out onto the field to revive an athlete's flagging spirit, a Life Coach revives the spirit of anyone feeling pulled down by negativity.

There may come a time when you feel stuck or frustrated and can't see the potential of a situation. At those times, we often simply need a little push to reconnect. Life coaching can be that helping hand.

I am just like you in many ways. I have experienced anxiety, insecurity, feelings of hopelessness and a lot of other negative feelings. I learned, through much hard work, that bad habits can be broken and negative thoughts can be reversed. Who better to empathize than a person who has been there?

To share my thinking with you, I have written numerous articles on my blog (www.susankorwin.com) and have a huge fan following on Facebook (www.facebook.com/pages/Susan-Korwin-Life-and-Style-Consultant/72540337439). Because I get many personal emails and letters of appreciation from my readers, I decided to create a book based on my articles, which in turn are based on the lessons I've learned through life coaching. It's my way of sharing my hard-earned experience with my friends—including the many friends I've never met and the friends I know I'll meet in the future.

1

Troubleshooting:
What's Getting in Your Way?

For many of us, it feels as if there's something standing between us and our personal definitions of success and happiness. Each of us has so much potential inside, and it's really up to us to make the most of it. No one can do it for us.

This chapter looks at some of the things that may be getting in our way: low self-esteem, fear and worry, negative thinking, negative people and jealousy. If one of these situations is holding you back right now, know that you can overcome it!

Things happen to each of us at times that may seem horrible, painful and unfair. We face illnesses (our own or that of others), we embarrass ourselves, we make silly mistakes, we get into bad relationships. All of these situations occur to test our limits. Without these tests, life would be a smoothly paved straight road to nowhere. It would be safe and comfortable, but boring and pointless. You wouldn't learn a thing.

My guess is that when you reflect on the bad things that have happened to you, you find that you overcame most, if not all, of them. You certainly survived them. Do you see how overcoming those obstacles showed you your own strength and resilience, your ability to persevere? Most times, the painful things that happen to us truly make us stronger.

We weren't born with the obstacles that now stand between us and our happiness and success. Challenging experiences in our lives helped shape and influence these obstacles. But just as we overcame (or survived and thrived in spite of) those experiences, we can overcome the "limits" we perceive in our lives right now.

When I started writing this chapter, I envisioned a troubleshooting guide like you find in an owner's manual. If something's not working, you go to the troubleshooting guide and look up the problem you want to solve. This chapter works largely the same way. You may struggle with self-esteem but not jealousy. You may not worry too much but be drained by the negative people you face every day. Whatever you think is slowing you down, go to that section and take from it what you need.

You are unique, you are valuable and you are full of possibility. It's time to overcome what's holding you back and share your powerful gifts with the world!

Self-Esteem

Lack of self-esteem is the only thing that stops us from success. Each and every one of us has some kind of unique talent. Know that you're someone special, you matter in life and you can make a difference. Know that you have the power inside you to reach great levels of achievement. You just need to believe you can in order for you to do so.

We often think that our worth and esteem are based on our looks and work. These qualities are fleeting. What's eternal is who you are in heart and soul. Shift the meaning of your worth from outer to inner, and you'll stop trying to prove yourself. Know that you are already a beautiful being, deserving of love.

Whether or not anyone else acknowledges it, you have value! You are worthy, even if nobody else says so. If you begin to live with that perspective, you will begin to emanate a sense of well-being that others will like and want to be around. You don't have to try to be liked. Your own unique version of *you* will be sufficient. People may still prefer someone else over you, but they will have a greater sense of appreciation for you as you express a greater appreciation for yourself.

How your childhood affects your self-esteem

When I was little, all my relatives and the adult friends of my parents pinched my cheeks and told me how adorable I was. My freckles and short, curly hair were constant topics of conversation. It was all good, or so I thought. As soon as I entered kindergarten, the compliments I grew to expect turned into daily insults by the little boys who surrounded me. What happened? Why did my freckles that were considered beautiful by the adults turn into something ghastly according to my peers? Not only that, but my short, curly hair was also suddenly something to be ashamed of! Oh, how I wanted to be like the other girls who had long, silken hair and no freckles.

This was the start of feeling bad about myself, which only got worse throughout elementary school. The social occasions in school were a source of torment. "I'm not holding hands with her. She's got freckles!" was a statement I heard often. Can you imagine what that kind of remark does for the growing psyche of a child?

In junior high, things got a little better. I had a huge circle of friends and even a boyfriend, but the feelings of doubt about my appearance festered. My boyfriend lavished me with compliments (a huge feat for a boy of 13), but I couldn't understand why. In my senior year of high school, a funny thing happened. I was driving and stopped to fill up my gas tank. When the time came to pay, the attendant smiled at me and said, "No charge for you. Your freckles are so beautiful, and they made my day." You could have knocked me over with a feather! Was he speaking to me?!? From then on, I found the tide had shifted. All of a sudden, all the things the little boys thought were ugly about me, the grown up boys thought were beautiful. My curly hair became "amazing" and the freckles were "sexy!"

The point of my story is, we don't realize how our early childhood affects us for the rest of our lives. I still feel a little shocked when I get complimented. Even after all these years.

A great number of adults can remember being the target of insults from their childhood peers, or being the one that targeted the other kids. Those who were initiators have, in all probability, shrugged it off as part of being a kid. However, for the victims, there are often deep scars. It's virtually impossible sometimes to know who suffers from low self-esteem; because the damage was done so early in life, they've usually learned how to hide it. But the truth is that they're usually terrified of failure, and often they are their own worst critic.

Through the years, I have learned to love myself. It didn't happen over-night. Here are some of the things that helped:

I take great care of myself. I get enough sleep, eat healthily and exercise consistently.

I maintain a list of my positive traits and accomplishments. I refer to it whenever I get "down" on myself.

I remind myself that I would never, ever want to hurt someone's feelings by making fun of them. This makes me a good person.

I try to avoid people and situations that are negative.

If you believe that someone you know suffers from low self-esteem, actions speak louder than words:

Always treat others the way you would want to be treated.

Pay compliments often. You can change someone's day!

Tell them how grateful you are that they are here in your life.

Make note of their accomplishments.

Don't ever insult anyone, even out of anger.

Most importantly, if you have children, teach them these rules early on. It doesn't take much effort to change someone's life profoundly.

The story of the two pots

This wonderful story is from an anonymous author:

A water bearer in India had two large pots. Each hung on the ends of a pole which he carried across his neck. One of the pots had a hole in it, while the other pot was perfect and always delivered a full portion of water. At the end of the long walk from the stream to the house, the cracked pot arrived only half full. For a full two years this went on daily, with the bearer delivering only one and a half pots full of water to his house.

Of course, the perfect pot was proud of its accomplishments. But the poor cracked pot was ashamed of its own imperfection, and miserable that it was only able to accomplish half of what it had been made to do.

After two years of what it perceived to be bitter failure, it spoke to the water bearer one day by the stream. "I am ashamed of myself. Because of my flaws, you have to do all this extra work. You don't get full value from your efforts," the cracked pot said.

The bearer said to the pot, "Did you notice there are flowers only on your side of the path, but not on the other pot's side? That's because I have always known about your flaw. I planted flower seeds on your side of the path, and every day while we walk back, you've watered them. For two years I have been able to pick these beautiful flowers to decorate the table. Without you being just the way you are, there would not be this beauty to grace the house."

Each one of us has our own unique flaws. We are all "cracked pots." But it's the cracks and flaws we each have that make our lives together so very interesting and rewarding. You've just got to take each person for what they are, and look for the good in them. We are all perfect—flaws and all!

How low self-esteem affects us physically

Feeling bad about yourself produces physical effects. People with low self-esteem tend to walk around with stooped shoulders, heads down, avoiding eye contact. A slumped appearance such as this portrays an image of someone uncomfortable and unworthy.

If this sounds like you, try this: Go for a short brisk walk somewhere you're not well known. Stand tall, make eye contact with people and give them a cheery hello. I did this very thing during the summer in Central Park! I smiled at every person walking past me. It automatically produced a chain reaction. They smiled back and said hello.

How you see yourself is how others see you. If you believe you have nothing to offer, others will pick up on this. If you feel you are worthwhile with plenty to offer, others will pick up on that. If you aren't convinced of your worth, how will others be convinced?

To reverse low self-esteem, your efforts must include standing up straight and looking ahead, not down. It's not only healthier but also displays confidence. Make a conscious decision to correct your posture, look people in the eye and change your image! Don't hide in corners or sit in the back. Let your presence be known.

Seek approval from yourself, not from others

> You have been criticizing yourself for years and it hasn't worked. Try approving of yourself and see what happens.
> —Louise L. Hay

One of the biggest obstacles to improving self-esteem is constant need for approval by others. People with shaky self-esteem feel that unless someone tells them what a great job they did or how wonderful they are, they're just not good enough. They don't believe in themselves, so they need to find someone else who will.

The problem is that it will never matter what someone else says because the most important person doesn't believe it: YOU! You'll always be looking for more and more people to affirm that you're valuable.

Most people look to others for clues about whether they're doing the right thing, wearing the right clothes, thinking the right thoughts, etc. There are others who, instead of looking outside to know if they're on the right page, look inside to figure out if everyone else is on the right page. Your voice is the one that counts. If your inner voice is making the decisions in your life, you'll be more powerful and charismatic.

An inner war often goes on inside us. It's the conflict between how we see ourselves and how others see us. In order to build self-esteem, you need to focus on your own self-worth from deep within. Only you know who you truly are. There will always be people who want to bring you down and who may hurt you with their rude comments. Their opinions don't count. Be strong and listen to your positive inner voice. The greatest and most ethical people have had their share of critics, but they didn't allow those critics to halt their success. Confidence must come from only one source and that is within you! Notice when you allow outer circumstances or the opinions of others to chip away at your self-confidence. Stop yourself and realize that no one has the power to validate you except you. Never let anyone's words, actions or perceptions affect how you view yourself or your worth. You own your life, and it's up to you to influence your own value and sense of well-being.

Ironically, even if a million people say wonderful things about you, you'll best remember the one person that made a negative comment. How many times have you been hurt because of someone else's opinion of you? When we experience self-esteem only through the eyes of others, one unkind word can shatter our sense of self. One unkind word. That's giving others a lot of power over your happiness!

Self-talk when others talk

Do you let others' opinions dictate how you feel about yourself? Don't worry, we're all guilty of it. Overcoming it just takes practice and the right self-talk. Consider these two thoughts:

First, what people say tends to be more about them, their beliefs and desires and hang-ups, than anything to do with you. We all get insulted, but when you realize that someone's words are a truer reflection of him or her and not you, it's easier not to take those words so personally.

What if the insult hits particularly close to home? What if you fear there's some truth to it? Don't internalize those critical comments. Consider them at a distance, with emotion out of the picture. Is there any truth to what was said? Do you agree with what was said, or do you know things to be different? If there's any nugget of insight in the insult, take it—otherwise, throw those comments away.

Second, two people will not necessarily see things the same way. I've seen two people in an art museum standing in front of a Rembrandt, each with a different opinion on whether he has any talent! Whatever people might think, say or do, realize that it's just their personal opinion. That's why you can't let what others think about you put pressure on you. Instead, love yourself as the masterpiece that you are!

Jack Canfield and Mark Victor Hansen, creators of the Chicken Soup for the Soul books, came up with a great acronym: "SWSWSWSW." This stands for "Some will. Some won't. So what? Someone's waiting!" In other words, some people will love what you do. Some will look at your work, your résumé, your art, and they'll just shrug and say, "Eh." So what? Somewhere out there, someone is waiting for your gift. So, step outside yourself and don't waste precious energy on what others think!

Self-respect is being able to stand tall and feel proud of and for ourselves. It's the foundation upon which other personal attributes are built ... honesty, confidence and integrity. Life's ups and downs have an impact on our self-respect. Some go with the flow and others get snowed under. By being dishonest and cheapening ourselves, our coating of self-respect will be chipped away. Others may show respect for us, but, self-respect is not gained from others ... it comes from within. Only we know who is looking back at us in the mirror. Be proud of that image.

We tend to be blind to our own greatness. We look at others and to others for self-assurance when, in reality, we have everything we need for greatness already. It's all within us, waiting to be noticed. And we're the only ones with the power to unlock it; no one else has the key!

Our self-worth doesn't depend on how many contests we win or how many parties we're invited to. Rather, we gain self-worth and character in how we lead our lives and the decisions we make each and every day. In reality, we're not going to win any gold medals for our hard work; there are no grand prizes for living a life of integrity. These decisions are made in order to fill ourselves with joy and self-respect. The saying, "It's not whether you win or lose, but how you play the game" holds true for life. The greatest prize of all is your dignity, and that comes with doing your best each and every day!

SUE SAYS

I believe in you, but my opinion is worth nothing. Everybody's opinion is worth nothing. Work on believing in yourself and letting go of needing others to believe in you. As soon as you start believing in yourself, others will start believing in you, too. But first, you must let go of needing their belief.

The perfectionism problem

Perfectionists expect to be top-notch at everything they do. It's great to have high standards, but when it leads to endless self-criticism and anxiety, perfectionism becomes damaging. Perfectionists are constantly worried about meeting their own unrealistic expectations and are constantly discouraged when they feel that they are not perfect. Once in a while, when they do allow themselves to feel satisfied, it usually doesn't last. "I could have done better" is a common phrase from the perfectionist's inner critic. Today, try to celebrate whatever you did well or even just good enough. After all, it's better to be a diamond with a flaw, than a pebble without one.

A few years ago, when my car was brand-new, I parked it in the garage. When I came around to the other side, I noticed that one of my kids had left his bicycle in a precarious position. As if in slow motion, I tried to keep it from falling over, but couldn't stop it. It fell right onto the side of my brand-new car, making a dent. This immediately caused me distress. Now my perfect car was flawed! I couldn't wait to get it to the body shop so that it could be perfect again! I reacted poorly, I admit it. I couldn't get that slight imperfection out of my mind, even though the car still functioned as it was meant to. I decided to shift my thinking then and there. In reality, who (except me) was going to notice that my car had a slight dent? It was still a beautiful car. How often do we spend our time focusing on the dents in our lives—those things that aren't perfect? How about when we focus on those people in our lives who aren't perfect? How often do we get caught up in the flaws we see? How often do we sabotage relationships because we don't look beyond the dents? Realize that we all have dents. There is no perfection. Acknowledge what is going right in your life . . . take your focus off the DENTS. If you do this, you will find peace and happiness.

Perfectionism is rooted in the desire to be accepted. Perfectionists run from one project to another, always looking for the applause and acceptance they need like a drug. Even when they get the praise, their perfectionism creates anxiety and makes each day stressful. In addition, perfectionists usually have trouble creating close relationships. When you are never satisfied with yourself, you can never rest. The sad thing is that, in the end, the lives of perfectionists are run by other people—the people they hope will approve of them if they are perfect enough. The cycle never ends. Today, give yourself a break. Stop the perfectionist cycle by focusing on what's important in life. It's not about being perfect, it's about being perfectly imperfect! After all, would you rather eat an apple that is shiny and perfect on the outside but rotten on the inside, or the one that is a little discolored and bumpy, but sweet and juicy on the inside?

Anxiety and stress, in some cases, are positive feelings—they encourage us to focus and prepare for urgent situations. I used to have major general anxiety disorder. I would wake up during the night and have to turn on the television to blur out my worries about "what ifs." In my case, the urge to prepare was exaggerated in my unrealistic quest for perfection and control. Through hard work, I have learned to manage those feelings, and one way was learning to live with imperfection. Also, being anxious takes lots of energy. I now use that same energy to do something productive such as exercising or dancing for an hour a day. I now have less energy available to be anxious!

When we compare ourselves to others, it's always to either celebrities we see in magazines or the person we know who seems to have it all—the best body, the fanciest car and the most friends. We set unreasonable expectations by comparing ourselves and asking why we can't be like that. We place a burden on ourselves by expecting another person's mold of perfection to fit into our mold. If we don't fit, we consider ourselves a failure and our negative self-talk becomes worse. There is nothing wrong with looking up to and aspiring to be like a positive role model. The problem lies in our emphasis on fitting into an unrealistic vision that is not us and will never be us. Let go of this perfect image and create visions of yourself as the best *you,* whether you aren't perfectly proportioned, whether you don't make a fortune of money and whether you only have a few friends. When you become comfortable with who you are, your mood will improve, your relationships will improve, and don't be surprised if people start wanting to be like you!

Remember, the approval you really need to find is within yourself. And you'll only find it once you stop searching for approval in others and take time to heal yourself. Often, even just the awareness of your actions will provide you with a great deal of healing. The moment you realize you don't need anyone else's approval is incredible. There's a peace inside which will make you absolutely joyful. You're now free to just be you.

Put yourself first

There are many people who depend on you daily: your spouse, your children, your friends. Imagine for a minute, putting yourself first.

Sounds selfish, but it isn't. Putting yourself first is not about abandoning others; it's simply about honoring your own well-being. How can you give all you're capable of if you aren't properly nourished, rested, happy and well? If you don't love and respect yourself, how can you expect others to do the same?

Truth is, you are useless to others if you don't take care of yourself first. On an airplane, you are instructed, should oxygen masks deploy, to put your mask on first so that you can help others around you. It's good advice for living on the ground, too. Don't let yourself go, because there are people who need you in their lives.

Do the things that show you care for yourself. Eat foods that serve your body. Get rid of the junk food and replace it with healthy alternatives. Drink plenty of water. Get enough sleep. Exercise regularly. Make time and space for fun. Stay focused on your vision and intention. Take care of your health. You can't help but feel better about yourself when you have the sense of accomplishment that comes from doing good for your body and spirit.

Be very kind to yourself. Who says kindness should only be given to others? No one deserves your kindness more than you do! Robert Holden in his book *Happiness Now* says, "In all my years, I have never had a client who suffered from being too kind to themselves!" Go on and pamper yourself, love yourself and give yourself a great big thank you for all that you are!

Putting yourself first is also about seeking love inward rather than outward. Falling in love with yourself can be just as wonderful an experience as falling in love with someone else. It's not conceited or selfish but a powerful act of self-love! Once you begin to love yourself unconditionally, your perspective will change. You'll start looking at yourself through fresh eyes, realizing the uniqueness of you. In turn, you'll treat yourself more lovingly, the way you'd treat anyone who is special to you.

If this feels odd to you, start small. Take 30 minutes each day to nurture yourself. You choose how. Read a treasured book. Take a nap if you need one. Soak in a warm bath. Exercise in any form, such as a walk in the park or even in place, is a particularly great way to begin. If 30 minutes of nurturing is too much, take 10 minutes and work up from there. By doing this, you're creating a routine which will eventually lift your spirit.

When you learn to embrace yourself with appreciation and affection, you begin to see the goodness and light that is within you, and gradually you'll realize you are worthy of respect from yourself. When you recognize your limits but still embrace life with gratitude, your sense of inner dignity will grow. You become less dependent on the affirmation of others and less troubled by the negativity of others.

You are a beautiful person with so much to share with the world. Honor yourself and make YOU a priority!

SUE SAYS

How would you treat a child, a close friend or a significant other that you truly loved? You'd go out of your way to support, care for and encourage that person. Well, why don't you treat yourself the very same way? You are just as important and deserving of excellent care as the people you hold most dear.

Challenge and throw away your labels

When I was in sixth grade, we had a required class in which we had to sew outfits to wear at our elementary school graduation. I quickly found out that sewing was not my strength, and every week when my teacher would check my progress, I would be ridiculed for my sloppy work.

One day she said, "Susan, you obviously don't have the talented hands that your mom has." (My mom was an artist.) So I gave up. I asked a friend to finish my outfit. And from that day on, when asked whether I had the talent that my mom had, I answered "no"—even though when I doodle on a piece of paper, everyone looks in awe at how great my work comes out!

I met someone who told me he didn't go to college as a young man because his dad always told him that no one in their family could go, because they weren't smart enough. So he never even applied! I told him he could break his family's life-long record by going now. He's now in his second year and doing great.

What's my point? We're all labeled at some point in our lives. "Too short to play basketball." "Too poor to make it out of the ghetto." "Not smart enough to make it into that college." The great news is, we don't have to accept these labels. We can tear them off; we don't have to wear anyone's opinion of us. We have the power to discard these outdated ideas that prevent us from being the best we can be. Wayne Gretzky, a phenomenal hockey player, was told he was too short to ever be successful. He didn't accept that self-limiting belief, and look where it got him!

Every time we have a limiting belief about ourselves, such as, "I'm never going to be successful," "My heart is going to be broken," "I'm ugly," we gradually paint a portrait that assumes to be who we really are. We go through our life looking at this portrait and hating it more and more. What we don't realize is that we are the artists who created that portrait! Remember this: If we can create a painting, we have the power, talent and capability to change it. Go ahead and take the paintbrush in your hand, revise your portrait, and see the beautiful and talented person that really belongs there!

So many times, after a moment of disappointment or a failed try at something, we label ourselves as losers or dumb. For instance, the other day I saw some photos of me taken at a party. They weren't very flattering shots, and my first thought was, "Boy, am I ugly"! But then I remembered all the good shots of me that I've seen. Sometimes you may take a not-so-great picture, but sometimes you look fabulous. A few bad shots don't make you ugly. Challenge negative thoughts by replacing them with positives. You may have failed at one, or even several, attempts, but it doesn't make you a failure.

Growing up, our self-image was based on what was programmed into us by others. If you were told your nose is too big, you might very well go through life thinking you're ugly. By removing these tainted thoughts (they're just circumstances of your past), embracing what makes you different and being open to a constant state of improvement, you can learn to love yourself. And that's when life will truly start to work for you!

Ignore the naysayers

Unfortunately, the world is filled with folks, including our inner critic, who want to us to keep small, to play along and to stay in the background. When we listen to them by apologizing for who we are, or diminishing our contributions, thoughts or feelings, we squelch our authentic selves.

Throughout our lives we are taught that praising ourselves is selfish and egotistical. But praising ourselves is something that nourishes our self-worth and causes us greater happiness which, in turn, spreads to others. Think of something—no matter how small—that you like about yourself. Give yourself the praise you deserve, just as you would a friend. Every time someone compliments you, write it down or remember it for later. When you get home, put the note in a box labeled "Great Things About Me." After a while, the box will get fuller and fuller. Whenever you get down, look at the notes and remember how wonderful you truly are.

If someone makes you feel that you don't rate, that's their problem. Never lose sight of who you are. Make a list of all your good qualities, habits and achievements. Believe in and accept yourself as you are, and never let anyone tell you who you should be. Stand in front of a mirror and write down what you see—not just your features, but what you see in your soul. Know that you deserve to be all of you, dazzling and one-of-a-kind. And never apologize for it!

I admit that I come from a long line of negative thinkers and worriers. I guess you can say it's in my genes. Hearing and experiencing the ways of negatively charged people over many years teaches us to behave and react in the same negative way. For many years, I used this as an excuse whenever I would ruminate about "what if's" and worst-case scenarios. Then I realized that having a predisposition to a certain behavior is not a terminal disease. It *can* be overcome. It took me a long time to change my automatic reflex to look at the dark side instead of the light. I still struggle with this. The habit of negative thinking can be so deeply ingrained that we fail to notice our constant application of it in our daily life. Often it is simply lack of awareness, outdated beliefs and habit. Most of the negative thinkers I know have no idea that this is their usual way of thinking and that negative thoughts have become part of their personality. Like any bad habit, you must retrain yourself away from negative thinking. Keep a journal and write down every time you have a worry or negative thought. Then write down the worst-case scenario next to your worry. After a while, when you look back over what you wrote, you'll realize that you're repeating the same worries and thoughts and that they never actually were as bad as you imagined.

Develop self-respect

Self-respect doesn't come from applause or outside attention. It comes from sticking to your values. When we lie, cheat or gossip, we tear at the fabric of our values. Every time you act in a manner that's true and upstanding, you increase your respect for yourself, you feel a sense of pride and you walk a little taller!

It's amazing how great it feels to do the right thing. The other day, I was paying for groceries and the cashier didn't see a large item I left in the cart. I could have walked away, but I pointed out that she forgot to charge me. She was amazed that I was so honest, and I walked out with a sense of pride!

Part of developing self-respect is being your most authentic self. It requires not following what everyone else is doing or thinking and, instead, being true to what feels right for you, even if it doesn't fit the needs and sensibilities of other people. It's not always easy, but we usually know what's the best action to take for ourselves. Self-respect encompasses being committed to being YOU, even when it seems scary and even when others may frown upon it.

When you want to change something about yourself

Would you marry or go out on a date with yourself? Would you hire yourself? Would you invite yourself to your own party?

If your gentle, honest (not self-flagellating) answer is no, consider the reasons why. Then, do something about it. Be what you want to attract into your life. Hit the gym and burn the fat. Instead of being the wallflower, use social occasions as a chance to meet new people. Find a new hobby to learn. Set a few new goals and celebrate when you reach them.

When we feel self-doubt, it's like constantly walking through a dark room with no flashlight. We wait for others to lead the way because we don't believe that we are capable or worthy. Confidence, like a light in a dark room, can lead the way. Please . . . look within yourself for that sliver of light. It's there, I promise you! It is then you will find the faith in yourself to move past your self-doubt. Shift your focus from what your mind is telling you to what your heart is calling out!

Each morning spend a few minutes visualizing yourself as the person you strive to be. Think about how you dress, how you carry yourself and the way you interact with other people. Seeing yourself as the person you want to become is a first step toward building self confidence.

Yes you can! Sure, it's easy for me to say that to you, and I truly believe it, but you're are the one who has to look in the mirror each morning and say to yourself, "Yes I can"! Start somewhere. Envision what you desire. When you're planning a trip, you get the map, plan your itinerary, then start traveling. It's the same for your goals. You can do anything you set your mind to, and don't let anyone tell you otherwise. You are a winner, you are talented and Yes You Can!

If you feel that something is off but aren't sure what, ask a trusted friend or relative what changes they think would benefit you. But be ready to accept their response! The automatic reaction to criticism, even when you ask for it and even when it's constructive, is defense. In this instance, rather than defend, listen for any truth behind the criticism. You can only change what you are aware of.

It's so hard for some of us to truly be who we are because we have been trained all our lives to live up to an expectation that the world believes is correct. We must begin to be content with ourselves and stop trying to change in order to fit into a certain social group. Stop caring about what people think of you. It really doesn't matter. If you're always concerned about whether people think you're good-looking, funny, fat or skinny, it's impossible to be yourself. If you change yourself to fit into one group, you will have to continue changing to fit into another group down the road. It will never end.

Be sure that you're initiating changes because you want the results they will bring into your life—not because you need to change to feel worthy or to fit in. We tend not to love ourselves unconditionally. We think we have to achieve something, obtain something or look a certain way in order to be good and deserve love. If you want to get an MBA, great! A fancy car? Fine! But don't think for a moment that you need these in order to have value as a person. Don't think you have to win at something in order to deserve self-love. At your core, you are great already!

Act without fear of failure
If you want to make a change, reject the self-doubt, the inward criticism of yourself and criticism of others. Be open to new ideas and realize that you need to break out of your comfortable habits. Take action. And remember that it's okay to fail.

It's common to be afraid of change because we're unsure of the outcome. Fear of the unknown prevents us from achieving self-improvement. Fear of failure keeps us from leaving our comfort zone. But change of some kind is inevitable. Rather than procrastinating, embrace the adventure of change. If you fail today, it doesn't mean you'll fail tomorrow. Change for the better, and in the process you'll gain the self-esteem you deserve.

I like to think of a baby who is learning to walk. He may fall, but he'll get up again and keep going. If he stopped, he'd never walk. Think of every failure as a step toward success.

SUE SAYS
Never compromise when it comes to your values. Every action has a reaction and only you are accountable. I believe that

people should behave in a dignified, self-respecting manner and take pride in themselves. When you look in the mirror, know that you have acted to the best of your ability, and at the end of the day, your sense of accomplishment will rival no other feeling.

Stop comparing yourself to anyone else because you are incomparable!

Society and the media seem to demand that we compare ourselves with others. We're often made to feel that we are, in some way, lacking or not good enough. Comparing yourself unfavorably to someone is the quickest way to put a halt to your growth of confidence. It is a waste of time and often damaging. No one has the perfect life, whether they have beauty, money or fame. Don't put other people on pedestals.

It only seems like your peers have it all figured out, that their challenges are less, their friends are better and their grass is greener. If only you could hear how much they admire you!

Remind yourself over and over why you like yourself. If you must compare yourself with someone, make sure it's a person who inspires you, someone who possesses the qualities of confidence that you're building for yourself. Break the habit of comparing yourself to others and realize how lucky and blessed you are in comparison to many other people in the world.

It takes much more courage to be true to yourself than to let others define you or to follow a crowd. The most successful people go with their instincts and, even if their choice is not a popular one, they stick to their principles. In a nutshell, always be your genuine self and follow your own value system. Stand up for what you believe and stick with it.

What is your gift?

Every person is born with unique talents, traits they're naturally good at or abilities that set them apart from others. When you find them and use them, these gifts lead to real happiness and success. Think about Michael Jordan. Born to play basketball. No matter how much you practice, you may never be as great as he was; he has a gift. You have gifts, too. Start noticing the compliments you often get from people. There's sure to be a gift there.

A lot of our insecurities come from focusing on things we have trouble with. The truth is that everyone has strong and weak points, but successful people have learned how to play up their good points, a skill that has helped them blossom. Despite insecurities, you have achieved a certain level of success in your life because you have great qualities. It's your job to pinpoint and harvest those qualities!

If we concentrate on our abilities and play to our strengths, appreciation of these skills will cause any inferior feelings we may have to be transformed into well-deserved pride. Our confidence will soar. And once we recognize our own inner talents, others will also.

Don't diminish your achievements. Embrace them and take pride in every single accomplishment. For instance, if someone tells you that you did a great job, don't say, "It was nothing." Realize that you worked hard and prepared for a positive outcome. Give yourself the credit you deserve for every aspect of your life—you'll create a positive outlook and increase your self-esteem.

Rebelling against your flaws will get you nowhere. Self-pity will get you nowhere. You must be adventurous enough to accept yourself as a bundle of possibilities and undertake the most challenging game in the world—making the most of your potential.

A special message for teen girls

I can tell you from experience that the teen years are a roller coaster ride of physical and emotional changes. These changes can fill you with self-doubt if you don't already have a positive body image. It's all too easy to be hard on yourself.

Unfortunately, physical appearance is the main factor that controls self-esteem at your age. If you don't feel attractive according to what the media portrays, or what your peers perceive as ideal, you may see yourself as worthless. Images in magazines and television are unrealistic and usually unobtainable. Extreme reactions to trying to become these images can result in eating disorders and other destructive, self-sabotaging behavior.

Some of you may feel you need to change how you look or act in order to feel good about yourself. Always remember that no matter what size you are, what color your eyes are or what color your hair is, you are unique! Everyone (even celebrities) has something they cannot change. Your height and the size of your shoes are examples. You can, however, set positive goals for yourself in order to improve something you *can* change. If you're eating lots of junk food, make it a goal to add a healthier alternative. Make a plan to exercise every day. Setting goals can help you feel in control of your life. This, together with a positive attitude and healthy lifestyle, builds your self-esteem from the inside out.

Here are a few tips that I recommend for you:

Always smile. A smile projects a friendly and winning attitude. It really is your best accessory. Even if you don't feel like it, forcing yourself to smile will lighten your mood.

When you talk to people, always make eye contact. If you're looking at the floor or around the room, you immediately project an image of low self-esteem. Let others know you are approachable and confident.

Volunteer your time to help others. Giving of ourselves is one of the quickest ways to gain self-esteem. This can be a nursing home, an animal shelter or any charitable cause. When you help others, you are also helping yourself!

Remember your posture! Good posture not only improves the way you look, but also helps you feel less stressed. Standing tall projects a positive self-image.

Always try your best and don't procrastinate. If you try your best and still don't succeed, don't be too hard on yourself. We learn from every mistake and failure.

Remember that nobody in this world is perfect. Everyone feels insecure at times, even if you can't see it from the outside. When you notice that you are saying negative things to yourself, put the brakes on!

You have so many great qualities; focus on them. Every morning, stand in front of the mirror and tell yourself what you will accomplish today. Give yourself a compliment. Maybe you have beautiful hair or amazing eyes. Focus on your assets. In the evening, look in the mirror again and list everything that gave you pleasure during the day. Maybe someone laughed at your joke, or maybe you held a door for someone. By concentrating only on the positive, you'll slowly change the way you feel about yourself. You'll realize what a special human being you truly are!

Fear and Worry

There are three types of fear: real fear, imagined fear and worry.

Real fear is healthy and can keep you safe. It's your intuition or your gut telling you something's not right. For instance, being afraid to purchase a new car when your finances are low is a healthy fear.

On the other hand, imagined fear (fear that's just in our heads) and worry (fear of something in the future) are not healthy. They are energy-draining and can be paralyzing. When we spend our time being afraid of perceived threats and worrying about unknown outcomes, we don't move forward. These kinds of fears are counterproductive and point-less. And most of the time, the things we obsess over and worry about never even happen!

Even though feeling fear is never comfortable, it's not always a bad thing. Sometimes when you feel afraid, it gives you the chance to figure out what exactly is holding you back. In this way, fear can be your guide, a signal from your subconscious that something's not quite how you want it to be. Instead of just feeling afraid, spend a little time thinking about your fear, and you may discover your true feelings beneath.

Never let fear dictate your life. It can be your greatest enemy, holding you back from success, happiness and fulfillment. Instead, use it to grow. Use it to change what's not working or what you don't like about your life. If you face your fears instead of hiding from them, you will grow—and happiness and success will follow!

Dealing with the fear of failure

When you were a kid, if you played a game and fumbled, did you shout "Do over!" and get another try? What ever happened to that magic eraser? Did we lose it, or did it simply fade away over time? Every day is full of the potential to make mistakes. When did we start taking every mistake—so minor in the grand scheme of things—so seriously?

Fear is a powerful and intense emotion, and it keeps many of us from improving our lives. Is fear of failure preventing you from moving forward? If so, then you must realize that failure is not your enemy.

We learn our best lessons from our failures. We learn more about our-selves when we fail than when we succeed. It makes us stronger and gives us character.

Our memories of past hurts and failures are extremely powerful. Each time a situation triggers a bad memory, we almost feel like we are reliving the experience all over again. When this happens, remind yourself that you survived whatever it was that hurt you. Visualize this bad memory floating away like a bubble and then bursting in mid-air. On the flip side, if you are worrying about future problems and thinking catastrophic thoughts, instead of thinking on the negative side, think of the best-case scenario for a change. A great outcome is just as likely as a bad outcome!

Frequently in life and in business, we get very comfortable and settle in to our programmed routines. But it's important to get out of our comfort zones to truly succeed and find our greatness. When you stay in one place without taking risks, you are limiting your potential. Successful people are those who conquer their fears.

When I was in college, I'd get so nervous when I had to stand up in front of class. So, I took Public Speaking. During this class, the teacher videotaped us and then pointed out our body language, unconscious habits, tics, etc. This was very intimidating for me, but in the end, it really helped me overcome my fear of talking in front of a crowd.

Sometimes doing something over and over—like giving a speech—builds your confidence. A mother eagle deliberately allows her eaglet to fall from the sky, swooping it up until it finally realizes that it has wings to fly. What does this say? It says that every obstacle in our path can teach us that we have the strength to overcome it. We just have to realize it!

Life is an emotional roller coaster, to say the least. Though the ups and downs aren't fun, keep in mind we must experience the bad to grow as individuals: we can't appreciate good times if we've never endured the bad. As you go, learn to take note of your successes and failures. Making a mistake isn't half as bad as repeating that mistake. And while you're at it, learn from the mistakes of others— and improve upon their solutions. Live, live, live . . . and learn!

What, me worry?

Blessed is the person who is too busy to worry in the daytime and too sleepy to worry at night.

—Leo Aikman

Fear and worry about the future can bring on depression, frustration, anger and other dark thoughts. In truth, the future rarely happens as we imagine it will be. But just like people, the more you feed your worries, the bigger they get!

One fall day, I had to go to an appointment I'd been dreading. There was no real reason why I needed to anticipate this event with fear, yet I worried for days in advance. Driving into Manhattan that day, the more I thought about my appointment, the more I played the worst-case scenario in my head. In general, when fear strikes, blood flows to the extremities, the legs and arms, preparing us to flee the dangerous situation. This is known as the "flight or fight" reaction. I could feel my heart beating, my mouth drying out, and for what? I was looking for a threat that wasn't even visible.

We all do it—ruminate. In other words, we obsess about a single doubt that gets caught in an endless loop of our thoughts. When we become too caught up worrying what the future may hold, we forget to live in the present. We operate in past and future and don't think about *now*.

I decided, while driving to my appointment, to switch my thinking to just the present moment. I concentrated on the beautiful Manhattan skyline and the changing colors of the leaves, which brought me into a more positive frame of mind. As it turned out, my appointment was a success. This is a common outcome when it comes to mindless fear and worrying. Usually the outcome is positive, yet we worried far in advance for no reason.

Worry is sort of like a muscle spasm: the mind clenches a thought and won't let go. You can't simply tell someone to stop worrying. They can't, as long as this "obsessive spasm" is tightening. The best way to stop the spasm is to replace it by thinking of past outcomes that resolved positively, even though you worried. The memory of the positive emotions will eventually release the spasm.

We will always be faced with worry in our lives. We just have to stay on top of it. When you realize that first small thought has grown into a full-on worry (or snowballed all the way into a panic!), grab the remote for your mind and change the channel to a musical or a comedy instead of horror movie!

Your best prevention is staying in the present. For example, give yourself the "assignment" of listening to the sounds around you; do that and you can't obsess about a fear or doubt. When you catch your thoughts traveling, bring them back. Once, when I was having some new flooring installed, I started ruminating about how much work I was going to have afterwards, when I would have to put everything back, vacuum, etc. I had to stop myself and decide to look at how beautiful everything was beginning to look *at that moment*.

If we could keep practicing this, we would be so much happier!

Words for worrywarts

If you are a constant worrywart, do this! Make a list of the things you worry about. Divide that list into two categories:

1. Worries or concerns that you can do something about.
2. Worries or concerns that are beyond your control.

Next to each item you can control, include an action step. For instance, if you worry about the weight you've recently gained, put together a plan to do something about it. If you're concerned about a deadline for a project, make a list of all the things required to get the project completed. Next to each item you can't control, write "NO WORRIES."

Make it a goal to conquer everything within your control and be consistent about not worrying about the things you can't. At first, it will be quite tough not to worry about the things you can't control, but with practice and self-discipline, it will become easier.

One of the traits of positive people is that they don't worry about things they can't control.

If the words "what if" crops up more than a few times a day in your thoughts, then I would say that you are a classic worrier. You feel that if you worry just enough about them, then you can control all those "what ifs" and then stop worrying. By not trusting in your capacity to handle life's curveballs, you "what if" in order to figure out what can go wrong, even before it happens.. You may have noticed that this doesn't work! Instead of stopping the worry, you have nothing but negative thoughts. Admit it, 99.9 percent of everything you fear will happen never does!

Always remember the difference between concern and worry. Concern is taking precautions because it's icy out . . . this is fact-based. Worry is thinking that a meteor is going to fall from the sky and hit you on the head . . . this is fiction-based. Whenever a worrisome thought arises, ask yourself, "Is this fact or fiction?"

I started doing a little worry ritual many years ago and it really works. Take an empty, vertical tissue box and write the words "Surrender Box" across it. Whenever you have a worry, write it down on a piece of paper, fold it up and place it in the box. You surrender the worry. The feeling is liberating! Months later, take a look at what you've dropped into the box. You'll be surprised at how many of these worries never came to be!

How to overcome your fears

Ground yourself in the present moment. When you're present, you're not thinking of what bad things can happen to you in the future or dwelling on the mistakes of your past. Stop, smell the air, notice the flowers blooming.

Don't dwell on your fears or your limits. We all do this sometimes, but if you catch yourself, *stop!* A perfect formula for an unfulfilled life is to accommodate self-defeating feelings while undercutting your finest, most productive ones. When doubts and fears want accommodations in your mind, turn on the "no vacancy" sign!

Face your experiences with an open mind. Life moves on, whether we act with courage or fear. Everything we close our eyes to and run away from defeats us in the end. When you keep an open mind, you may find joy and strength even in painful moments. Every experience is golden for those who have the vision to recognize it as such.

Believe in yourself and your capacity to handle whatever comes your way. Say that there are two roads ahead: Fear Street and Faith Street. Which road will you take? The answer is the positive road, paved with faith and a belief that your best days are not behind but ahead of you. With this belief, you'll make right choices today that will create your positive future tomorrow. Even if you still feel fear, focus on solutions instead of problems. You're stronger than you may think.

Keep trying new things. We tend to be afraid of things we're not very good at or have little experience with. If you're feeling fearful about something, what kind of education or practice can you take on, to diminish that fear?

Turn fear into growth

We often fear the unknown or change in our lives. This fear can stop us from moving forward. Don't let this to happen to you. Never changing is stagnation! Everyone's afraid of something—making a fool of himself or herself, failing, looking unattractive, saying the wrong thing, the list goes on! The key is to not let it paralyze you.

How do you know you like chocolate? You tried it. How do you know you like swimming? You tried that as well. Life is so short. We must seek out those experiences we've been thinking of but were too afraid to try.

How many of us, for fear of not being perfect, just sit out when it comes to pursuing our hopes and dreams? Woody Allen once said, "80 percent of success is just showing up." Do you think that someone with a great body just sits back and hopes to have the perfect body? No, she shows up at the gym every day and works hard to achieve it. I never became a concert pianist, but I still sit down every day and play the piano because I enjoy it. No one, and I mean no one, is perfect. If everyone sat back and didn't pursue success for fear of not being perfect, there would be no museums, no theater and no books to read! What makes a winner is someone who sticks with the game. When I pick the people I want in my life, I don't look for perfection . . . I look for the ones who show up!

One evening, I was watching with awe a group of dancers moving to the beat of a live Brazilian band. I was dying to get up there, but knew I had no idea what I was doing. I decided to challenge my fear of getting up on that dance floor; I said to myself, "Okay, fear, welcome to my world. Let's do this together!" I got up, started following the steps that others were taking, and before I knew it, multiple partners appeared. I was getting private dance lessons! Even though I kept losing my step, I had a blast. And I survived my fear!

You don't have to be fearless. Just realize that you can acknowledge the fear—and keep moving forward! Only when we are no longer afraid do we begin to live.

Remember, we all are afraid of something. Make a decision today to face at least one of your fears. You will see yourself growing into a more confident and purpose-filled individual.

Negative Thinking

Remember, the voice telling you that you cannot do something is always lying.

—Unknown

Are you infested with ANTs? No, not the crawling little insects that invade your pantry, but the Automatic Negative Thoughts that invade your thinking!

It took me years to grasp the truth that for better outcomes to happen, I needed to look within myself. I needed to learn to be a master of my thoughts instead of letting worries, doubts, fears and wild, aimless notions eat into my psyche.

The only lasting way to change your life and circumstances is to change your thoughts.

When your thoughts turn negative and destructive, they're like a scratched record playing over and over in your mind. You have to let the bad thoughts go and replace the record with songs that celebrate your greatness and a future filled with hope!

It's all about our inner dialogue. We must become more aware of what we say to ourselves, both consciously and unconsciously. And we must change what we say, instead of simply trying not to listen. When the negative self-talk appears, we must substitute positive words for the negative words.

Your thoughts ultimately affect your habits, character and circumstances. Please remember, you're special and unique, and you're here to walk a path only you can travel in this life. The power to change things resides in your mind and within you.

Negative thinking is a habit. Negative thinkers were either taught to think that way or conditioned themselves to think that way. In our society, we've developed the tendency to focus on minor irritations, even though these annoyances are only a tiny part of our overall lives. It's sad that we tend to focus on the five percent of our lives that is going wrong instead of the 95 percent that's going right! Stay focused on positive things. Read uplifting material, stay around upbeat and motivating people. If you have to watch the dreary news, keep it to a minimum. Remember, you may have missed the bus on the way to work, but, think about it . . . you get to go to work! There's always a positive spin on a negative situation. Focus on that!

Your thoughts control your destiny

I recently attended a function where raffle prizes were given away. As they were calling the numbers, the lady I was with said she knew she would win because she always does! I just smiled. Guess what? She won!

You get what you expect, and lucky people expect the best. These expectations become self-fulfilling prophecies. Ask around and you'll find that lucky and unlucky people have *very* different expectations.

The "dominant thought principle" says that our thoughts are pretty much directly linked to what we get in our lives. Think about what you say to yourself most of the time. Do you smile at the thought of how lucky you are to be healthy, or do you constantly wonder what disease could strike you at any moment? I know from experience that whenever I'm going to have my blood pressure taken, my heart immediately starts racing, and I envision myself having a terribly high reading. Now, most days, my blood pressure is just fine, but because my thoughts always go to that negative mindset, sure enough, I get the undesired result: elevated blood pressure!

What I did was plant the seed in my mind: I am going to have high blood pressure. My mind then dutifully went about fulfilling that thought.

We get what we expect. We act on our most dominant thoughts, so if we are constantly telling ourselves that we are not worthy, our mind will start believing it, and we will go nowhere.

This doesn't mean you can't think negative thoughts, or that they have to be totally eliminated from your life. That would be virtually impossible. Negative thoughts can still be there . . . just don't latch on to them. Let them float through and forget them. Notice what you focus on.

This also doesn't mean that if you focus your mind on becoming the best tennis player, it will happen just like that. No, if you really want to be a great player, become obsessed with the idea and then take action. Learn everything you can about the game and practice it, knowing that eventually you have the power to be great at it. We become what we think about, first in thoughts and then in action.

A lot of us are burdened with unresolved issues from our past that we just don't want to deal with. We may even deny they exist, yet they follow us wherever we go. In life coaching, we call this emotional baggage. When we drag around emotional baggage day after day, and year after year, these feelings pile up and we become overwhelmed. We may experience headaches, depression, high blood pressure and stomach ailments. By avoiding these issues and trying to be strong, we are, in fact, not living a life of happiness. When you delve into your feelings and really acknowledge what it is that's burdening you, you set yourself free from the emotional jail you placed yourself in. Having baggage isn't a sign of weakness—we all have some. Allow yourself to open up the bags and really look at what it is that you have been carrying around for so long. Then, toss all those things away! It's time for a new start.

You've heard the expression, "Pick your battles." If you really think about it, it takes a lot more energy to fight against something than to avoid the fight in the first place. One battle that can be avoided is the battle between you and your negative thoughts. Imagine this dark thought, whatever it may be, as an enemy that needs to be forcibly removed from your mind. But, like a schoolyard bully, the thought will just keep coming back to torment you. Here's another approach: Instead of shoving that thought out of your mind, acknowledge its presence, stay calm and confident, then tell the thought to move along. When the bully (your habit of negative thinking) comes back, look it straight in the eye and tell it in a peaceful way to leave your space. If you pick your battles, you don't need to get into a shoving match.

Keep your thoughts on the positive side: "I am so loved." "I am so lucky." "Great things are going to happen today." Generating dominant thoughts that are in line with what you want (rather than what you don't want) is a tool to bring about great changes in your life. Learn to implant thoughts in your mind that will benefit you. Envision your ideal self, so you can become what you think you are.

Life is like the echo you hear when you are standing in a canyon. If you yell, "Coward!" that's what will be repeated. If you yell, "Hero!" that's what will be repeated. If you want more harmony in the world, create more harmony in your heart. If you want more competence from others, improve your competence. This reciprocity applies to all aspects of life: life will give you back everything you give to it!

Perfect how you talk to yourself

Each of us has our own special saboteur, the voice in our heads that says, "You're not good enough." "Who do you think you are?" The saboteur's job is to protect you from taking risks and making changes. It affects the choices you make. But the voice isn't real, and what it's saying isn't true. Separate your true voice from the saboteur, and it will change your life.

How do you do this? Start by listening carefully to everything you say to yourself throughout the day. Only once you become aware can you change your self talk. When you hear yourself say, "Nothing is going right for me today," change it to "Today is a good day. I'm in control!" Do this and see how your day turns around. Your day will improve as your attitude improves. Monitor your self talk this way every day, and all your days will get better!

In the same way that washing your face and brushing your teeth keep your skin and mouth healthy, positive self talk keeps your mind and self-image healthy. The more you practice, the more natural it will feel to constantly offer yourself words of hope and strength, in spite of any external chaos. Eventually, your own voice should be the only thing you need to hear to spark your happiness and ambition.

Positive self talk is basically rewiring your internal computer. You've been programmed all your life to hear the can'ts instead of the cans, to remember the boos but not the bravos. And what is programmed into our brain becomes our dominant thought. However, through repetition you can eventually replace the old thoughts. Every time you hear your negative saboteur voice, replace it with an opposite, positive thought. It takes time, but eventually it will become a habit.

These opposite, positive thoughts are called affirmations. You can summon them in response to a negative thought, or you can say or write them specifically to change something in your life. If you want to lose weight, turn "It won't matter if I eat this just once" into "I'm pleased with myself. I'm not going to eat this." Say affirmations to yourself with emotion and importance.

In the past, no matter how many compliments I received, it was the perceived insult that stuck in my mind. Now I try to think and speak positive words to myself everyday. I'm sure you have at some point talked down to yourself. Negative self talk makes you feel hopeless and pessimistic.

I remember seeing myself in a video one day and hating the way I looked. I thought to myself how ugly I must be. I started to dissect every flaw I saw, finally reaching the conclusion that I look horrible. I wasn't the same the whole day until I realized that nothing had changed. My face didn't all of a sudden change. It was my perspective that changed. My inner critic was taking pleasure in pointing out all the ways I don't measure up. I decided not to allow this mean girl to attack me anymore. When I agreed with that negative voice, I gave it all my power. Okay, I said to myself, I may not be perfect, but I still love myself, flaws and all!

It's true that sometimes we are our worst critic. We must concentrate on all our good qualities (we all have good qualities) instead of focusing on what we perceive to be imperfections. I have a beautiful farmhouse table in my kitchen, and you know what I like the most about it? The fact that it has little deviations in the wood. To me, that's what makes it unique. We should all look at ourselves the same way.

When you lack control, control your reaction!

We have no control over 10 percent of what happens to us. We can't stop the car from breaking down or a storm from rolling in when we expected sun. The plane may be late, throwing our whole schedule off. A driver may cut us off in traffic. We've no control over this. But you determine the other 90 percent by your reaction. You can't control a red light, but you can control your reaction. In reality, a red light lasts 45 to 60 seconds. In the grand scheme of things, why stress? Use that time to take a deep breath!

You may not be able to stop the rain that falls into your life. This downpour can be so hard at times that we can't see where we're going. But we can turn on our windshield wipers (meaning, get some perspective) to clear away the frustrations, criticisms and self-doubts that, like a drenching downpour, can obscure our vision. When you're feeling upset, know that despite any storm, the sun will shine again.

Don't let a rude comment or a betrayal from a friend ruin your day. We don't always have a choice in what happens to us, but we always have a choice how we react to it. Never give anyone the opportunity to steal your joy. Don't give them that power, because your joy is your strength. You may be shaken for sure, but never let yourself get stirred!

In truth, we're the only ones who have control over how we feel going through our day. There will always be situations that can ruin a day, but nothing and no one has the power to control your reaction except you!

If past beliefs are weighing you down, let them go

When we were born, we were a clean slate with no opinion of ourselves. Along the way, through parents, teachers, neighbors, friends and even strangers, we were told of our limitations. We grew up with this self-defeating programming: "We are all overweight in this family, so you'll never be thin." "We're all addictive personalities, so you will be, too." "None of us ever became financially successful, so don't bother trying."

These false beliefs were heard enough in your childhood that they became an internal recording of sorts, playing over and over until the thoughts became a habit. Scientists calculate that the average adult has around 90,000 thoughts each day, of which 60,000 are repetitive. What are those repetitive thoughts telling you?

To experience the life you were meant to enjoy, take the necessary steps to unlearn the false beliefs from your past which are keeping you stuck in a perceived world of lack and limitation. How? Change the recording and you will change your life!

If you perceive yourself as common or of limited ability, you've simply formed a habit of thinking of yourself that way. And this habitual thinking will keep you stuck. You must form a better habit, for example, the conception of yourself as limitless in your power. It's habitual thinking, not periodic thoughts, that decides your destiny!

You don't feel guilty when you throw out the trash, so why hesitate to throw out your false beliefs? We all need to take inventory of our beliefs occasionally. Put them under the microscope and see which ones are valid: how you think about yourself, your place in life, others, your relationships, even life itself. If a belief no longer benefits you, it's time to let it go. We don't take out the trash or clean out the refrigerator just once; we do these chores again and again over time. It's the same with our thoughts and beliefs. If you toss out a false belief and then hear it popping back up again, say to yourself, "No, not true. I don't believe that anymore."

Keep working on changing those old, outdated beliefs about yourself. Before you become angry at the people who set your recording in motion, know that many false beliefs are originally created with good intentions— to keep you safe, to protect you from more pain and suffering, or to guide your expectations. But no matter how well-intentioned this information was, if these beliefs are no longer true (or never were true) or if they don't serve you anymore, you *can* change.

Here's a ritual that is known to work. Every day, three times a day, look in a mirror and say these words: "Every day, in every way, I'm getting better and better." Our subconscious mind is entirely reprogrammable by listening to repetitive messages, just as it was first programmed with false beliefs.

Negative or positive thinking becomes second nature to us, depending on which mental habit we have adopted over the years. Yes, that's what it is, a habit! It's what we have become accustomed to. Positive thinking is a good habit, one that doesn't need to be broken. But self-critical thoughts are something different. You can't just tell yourself to think positive. You must monitor and be aware every time a defeating thought enters your mind. Here's a tip I learned a while ago: Put a handful of paper clips in your pocket or purse. Every time you make a critical remark to yourself, link one paper clip to another. You may be shocked to see how long the chain is by the end of the day! Unchain your self-defeating thoughts. They are just standing in your way. Possibility thinking is your key to happiness and success.

Our background and circumstances may have influenced who we are, but we are responsible for who we become. Don't use any excuses to hold yourself back from success. We're capable of anything we put our minds to, even if we were told early on that we couldn't!

How to change your negative thinking

Switch your focus to success. Two objects can't occupy the same place at the same time. Put a brick in liquid and the liquid gets displaced. Two opposing thoughts are similar. You can't think of failure and success at the same time. So if you stop concentrating on failure and start concentrating on success, success will displace failure. Win or lose, it's *you* who decides.

Ask yourself, "What's the best thing that can happen?" Thoughts aren't little tidbits of information that enter our minds and turn to dust. Thoughts are concrete. Our words and beliefs shape our daily lives. So don't be a victim. You're worthy, and your dreams are within your reach. Imagine positive situations with happy outcomes. Instead of asking, "What's the worst that can happen?" expect the best!

Avoid negative people as much as you can. Surround yourself with people who encourage you. Negativity breeds negativity. Life is hard enough without being brought down by people who constantly see the bad in every situation.

Have a purpose. If you know what you are here to do and why you are here to do it, then the power of your purpose will be greater than any challenge or naysayer. Remember your purpose, tune out the naysayers and focus every day on being your best and bringing out the best in others.

We all are a mixture of positive and negative attributes. Not one of us is perfect or else we wouldn't be human. However, most of us tend to forget what's great about ourselves and instead focus on what we don't like about ourselves. Here's a great idea: Ask a few people you know (friends, relatives, colleagues) to write you a letter of recommendation. From the letters, you'll be able to observe how key elements of yourself—your personality, your work ethic, sense of humor, and so on—appear to others. You may find that what others see as positives about you may be qualities you have overlooked or forgotten. This is a great way to build your self-confidence, plus it will help you in your self-awareness. Sometimes, all it takes is hearing from others how wonderful you truly are!

Feed the positive. Imagine a little guy on each shoulder. One says how great you are. The other says you're a loser. Which one grows? The one you feed the most. Instead of thinking about what you don't have, think about what's great in your life. Two thoughts can't occupy the same place in your mind. Feed the positive guy, and he'll grow! You'll have more optimism, a stronger immune system and a happier you.

When you wake up feeling negative, think positive before you rise. Breakfast is essential fuel for people to function optimally. Just as important are the first thoughts of the day. Your first thoughts as you awake set the stage for your day. Are you thinking, "Grr, I don't want to get up. I don't want to go to work." Or "I'm going to grab a warm shower, put on my favorite sweater and treat myself to some coffee before work. I'm so lucky to have a job that pays all my bills." Feed your mind with positive thoughts and set the tone for the rest of the day.

If you are in a doom-and-gloom mood, redirect your focus to the many blessings in your life. Are you in reasonably good health? Can you see, hear and smell? Is there a roof over your head and enough food to eat? There are many people who are not able to enjoy these gifts and who would gladly trade places with you. Concentrate on the many things for which you are grateful. Here's an idea: Write down on the back of an index card, "Counting My Blessings," or "I have so much to be grateful for." List everything for which you are grateful, even the smallest things like your morning coffee. Place the card where you'll frequently see it, such as on your desk, in your car or on the bathroom mirror. By focusing on what you have instead of what you don't have, your energy will change direction from negative to positive.

Rephrase your thoughts. Do you tell yourself you have to go to work? Just change that one word to "get." You get to go to work. Or you get to go to the gym. It's not a chore, it's something you're lucky enough to get to do. By changing this one word, you will shift your mindset to feel better about an event or situation. Soon, you'll start to realize how lucky you really are! When you start to understand that these things we take for granted or dread are actually things some people only wish they could do, you realize how blessed you are. How many who are jobless would love to work today? How many who are disabled would love to get to a gym today? Put every-thing in perspective and your world will change!

How to break a bad mood

Exercise and get some sunlight. Do both at once if you can! Chemicals in the brain that control how we feel, like serotonin, dopamine and endor-phins, can be released by exercise and sun exposure.

Eat mood-boosting foods. Strawberries, chocolate, salmon and ba-nanas are all foods that can help you feel better. Even a cup of coffee in the morning releases those feel-good chemicals.

Let music take you back to a happier time. Researchers have found that music is an important influence on our memories. We associate songs with emotions, people and places we've experienced in the past. To this day, if I hear "She's a Woman" by the Beatles, I'm transported back to my first kiss. And I particularly love summer songs that bring back memories of being at the beach with my friends. This is why oldies stations are so popular. If you're feeling down, seek out the music that's the soundtrack for your happiest memories.

Wait 48 hours before you act on your bad mood. If you go out and shop to feel better when you're feeling blue, next time wait 48 hours before you buy. You'll have time to make sure you really want and can afford the item. If you get the item and then discover you can't afford it, your bad mood will soon return!

Act happy. Even if you are having a bad day, act yourself into reality. Acting cheerful can help trigger positive emotions. Adopt the stance of being a confident, happy, successful person and you'll grow into the role.

Harness your imagination for good

Use your imagination not to scare yourself to death but to inspire yourself to life.
> —Adele Brookman

You know the expression "Out of the mouths of babes?" Well, this is a true story about how my son taught me a lesson more than ten years ago, when he was young. I had to have a diagnostic test done and was completely obsessed with the thought of a negative outcome. I was already planning what I would do in the worst-case scenario. Finally, my son said to me, "Mom, you're so worried about dying, but right now you might as well be dead because you aren't living. Only worrying about dying."

Wow! I was jolted back to reality. He was right! Now, mind you, this medical test was just a routine test and everything turned out fine in the end. But because of my negative self-talk, I took a normal situation and made it worse.

My point is that we all think the worst from time to time. What's important is not to make a habit of it. When you catch yourself doing it, *stop* and replace your vision with more positive thoughts and outcomes.

Where is your focus, and what is your perception? I'll bet almost every terrible thing that ever happened to you mostly happened in your imagination. Think back over time about what things kept you sleepless at night. Try to recall all the things that really had you worried, scared or upset. How many actually happened? And of the ones that did happen, how many were as bad as you had imagined?

When your imagination dwells on pictures of doom and gloom, replace those pictures with positive ones. When something scary enters your mind, ask yourself "What's the best thing that can happen?" Focus on that! Most times, there are solutions to every problem or disaster that occurs.

Part of my training for Life Coaching was listening to CDs of positive self-talk affirmations. Each CD used repetitive sentences, such as "You are doing great" or "Be proud of today's accomplishments." When I listened to them, I usually was busy doing something else, but the words were always in the background. Our minds work in amazing ways. Even though the tapes were playing and I was doing something else, my subconscious portion of the brain soaked it in. What I am trying to say here is that by repeating positive words to yourself all day, either by listening to tapes or just saying them over and over, your mind will soak it in without you even realizing it. To put it simply, we must claim our dreams and believe that we are on the way to achieving them. We need to feed our minds with constant thoughts of "I can do it." Studies have shown that affirmations do work in helping us become more positive and achieving what we want. Athletes use them all the time before a big game. It's a winning strategy for them and it can be for you, too. Repeat words of encouragement to yourself as often as you can. Don't stop. Positive thoughts will eventually overtake the negative ones because our brain soaks in our dominant thoughts.

Often, no matter how hard we try, there will be problems that cannot be solved and are out of our control. When we encounter these types of problems, we need to recognize them for what they are and focus our energy on regrouping rather than butting our heads against a wall. Remember, if there *is* a solution to the problem, why be unhappy? If there *isn't* a solution to the problem, why be unhappy? Have a direction in life, set goals, and have the courage and confidence to move past the obstacles that block the way. If you don't move forward, you will fall behind. Happiness is meant to be found along the route—it's not some grand prize at the journey's end.

Thoughts of light

Imagine a room that's pitch dark and a room of bright light, both connected by a door. When you open the door from either side, what happens? Light floods into the dark room, illuminating it. Live accordingly: think thoughts of light.

People who soar are those who refuse to sit back, sigh and wish things would change. They don't beat themselves up, complain of their lot in life or dream of their ship coming in . . . someday. Rather, they use their minds in the best ways possible: to articulate their desires and their commitment to achieving those desires. To visualize their success. To remind themselves, again and again, that they are capable and competent. Use your mind in the best way possible, and in time you will live the life you really want!

Negative People

Treat everyone with politeness, even those who are rude to you—not because they are nice, but because you are.

—Unknown

Let's face it: Each of us has had bad things happen to us which cause us to become gloomy. Sometimes it can be a challenge to stay positive. Those who have healthy mindsets and an upbeat attitude usually are able to combat the negativity and turn their negativity into a positive outlook. On the other hand, there are those who always see the worst in every situation and don't hesitate to remind us of it. If we're not careful, these people will suck the life out of us, making us exhausted and, eventually, depressed.

I often wonder how negative people get to be that way. It certainly can't feel good to always see the glass as half-empty. Many times they are conditioned to be negative from the way they were raised. Other times, they've been hurt so much in the past that being negative is a way of protecting themselves from further hurt by keeping others at a safe distance.

Most of us have encountered negative people in our life: at the office, among family and friends, even the stranger sitting next to us on a train. Who, in your circle of friends, family and coworkers, brings you down and puts you in a negative state of mind? Even though you may really like these people, taking part in their "misery loves company" behavior will only deflate you and keep you from reaching your goals. Negative people are toxic. They can be as detrimental to our health as the chemical toxins we try to avoid. They drain our energy, raise our blood pressure and generally sap our strength.

That's why it's so important to surround yourself with the right people—those who want you to win and want to be winners, too! You are the average of the five people you spend the most time with. Folks who pull you away from your goals can cause you to become unbalanced. Those who tease you or make fun of your goals can become toxic to you. Good friends want to see you succeed; toxic friends are afraid of seeing you succeed, perhaps because it reminds them how they're not succeeding in their lives.

Can you remember a time that you had to deal with a negative, vindictive and difficult person? When was the last time someone said something with the intention of hurting you? Unfortunately, these people are everywhere and can't always be avoided. They want to get a reaction which, in turn, gives them power. It's very easy to want to attack back, but don't.

When we react to negativity, we disturb our own inner being and create pain within ourselves. No good can come out of reacting against someone who is bent on negativity. It will only trigger more anger and additional reaction from that person. Who needs this negative downward spiral? These people drain our energy. If you want to live a life with less stress, delete these people from your life. Avoid any interactions with them as much as you are able to. It's your choice who you choose to allow into your space. Stay around people with the qualities that you admire: positive, peaceful, encouraging and dignified. I guarantee you will feel washed, rinsed and cleansed!

Character traits such as depression, negative attitude and pessimism seem to have some genetic basis. But if we inherit these traits, are we stuck with them? Nature does play a role, but so does nurture. I believe that these traits are also learned and reinforced when we are constantly surrounded by people who act in a certain manner. I've seen whole families, including cousins, aunts and uncles, who possess the same traits, carried down from their grandparents and possibly even earlier generations. We can't control who our parents are, but we can realize that negative traits are also a habit. That means the chain can be broken, just as any habit can be broken. By refocusing your natural tendency to lean toward the negative, you will eventually re-train your brain to see the positive.

You can't change your past or the way you were brought up, but you can change who you spend your time with now. Make a list of the top five people you spend your time with. Next to their name, write either a P (for positive) or an N (for negative). Do they lift you up and encourage you? Or do they constantly whine and moan about everything and make you feel that nothing will ever work? Minimize your contact with the N types and you'll minimize the negativity in your life.

If there's one particular person in your life who's challenging to you because of a negative approach to problems, notice the next time you help how you feel afterward. Do you feel drained, tired or annoyed? If so, then all you've done is give your power and energy to that person. This is not beneficial to you, and it doesn't even help the person in the long run. Remember, you are not responsible for anyone else's life—you don't have to solve anyone's problems. Don't feel guilty for someone's unhappiness. Let go of trying to fix the problems; he or she doesn't want that anyway. They simply want your energy. At some point, we just have to let someone take responsibility for his or her own life. If we're constantly there to fix everything, the person will never grow.

How to respond to negative people

We all know Mr. and Mrs. Doom and Gloom. You can recognize them very easily. Here's what they're like:

They have a negative view of the world;
They complain all the time;
They criticize others on a regular basis;
They are the first ones to tell you that your goals will never work;
If they do laugh or smile, which is rare, it is only to make fun of others;
They are generally in limbo in their own life with no clear goals.

These people will suck the air out of the room and depress you in no time! I am here to tell you to stay away from them. I am also here to tell you that the world is still a wonderful place, and the economy, the environment, and everything else that Mr. and Mrs. Doom and Gloom are predicting will get worse, is going to get better. There are still many people with big hearts and many people who smile at others' success. Look for these people in the crowd. I know I do!!

Whenever a negative tirade starts, just smile and don't remark. Remain detached. Don't get involved in the conversation. If you can, get up and leave the room. Negative people feed on getting reactions. If you get caught in the web, your energy will start to drain.

Or listen to their story with empathy at first, and then offer a positive spin on whatever they're complaining about. Help them to see that every difficulty leads to change, growth and healing.

Offer solutions. Negative people usually see situations as completely hopeless, because they're focusing on problems rather than options. Encourage them by offering helpful solutions. Tell them they're powerful enough to change that bad situation into a good one.

Get perspective. Sometimes a person is negative because they're just plain unhappy. Maybe they hate their job, feel trapped in their marriage or lack self-esteem. They can only feel powerful by hurting others. If you can understand this person's problems, he or she may be easier to deal with.

A few years ago, someone said to me that we are all human magnets. I recently remembered that analogy when I encountered a very negative and toxic person. Negative people carry with them negative vibrations that can, if we allow it, attach to us like a magnet. But it's we who are the magnets, not the other person. By allowing ourselves to have a negative reaction, we attract negativity into our own life, resulting in stress and loss of sleep. If we ignore these negative influences, go on with our lives and stay with positive people and positive thoughts, we allow positivity to attach to our magnet. Some people call this the law of attraction. Whatever we call it, it really works. It's not always easy, but remember that it's not about the other person or the situation. It's about how you react to the situation and whether you want to allow their negative energy to repel or attract you.

> Keep your internal dialogue positive. If you're with someone who says, "You're not going to lose weight anyway, might as well not try," it's going to bring you down! Don't internalize what he says. If you must spend time with him, make sure to answer his statements with your own positive take. Think like a winner, which you are!

> It's virtually impossible to avoid allowing some negativity to enter your zone. However, just because someone (or a situation) is throwing negativity your way, you don't need to catch it or let if affect you emotionally. You can't swim in polluted water yet come out without any dirt on you. If you want to avoid the dirt of negativity, then refuse to take a dip into that river! Let it all go, and avoid people and situations that add negative drama to your life.

> If you can't change the people around you, change the people you are around. The more you seek quality and integrity around you, the easier it becomes to decide who gets to sit in the front row and who gets moved to the balcony of your life. Remember, the people we hang out with impact our lives. Stick with those who respect your dreams and ambitions. Don't share your dreams with negative people or feed your efforts with negative thoughts.

> We let go of negative and toxic people in our lives because their presence is undesirable and only causes us to catch their gloomy outlook. So, why is it that we keep holding on to our problems, stress and insecure thoughts? They are *not* our friends, yet we let them hang around us constantly. Get rid of those unwanted friends and commit to finding new companions to share space in your head.

Like attracts like, so practice staying positive and setting healthy boundaries. Negative people will either shift their attitude to match yours, or they won't be attracted to you and will move on. Then, you'll only be surrounded by other positive people!

SUE SAYS

Someone asked me once on my Facebook page why mothers-in-law always seem so negative and unsupportive. Here's my take: I think, in general, it's hard for them to be objective when their son or daughter is not under their influence or in their control anymore. That's how the cliché about in-laws came to be. Some can let go and others can't. The ones that can't become hostile when their opinion is no longer the only one that matters. It's hard for both sides—the mother-in-law's and the new spouse's!

Fortify your mind against negativity

Just as you have an alarm system for your home to keep out intruders, so should you fortify your mind from negative intruders. Select what you will allow in your life, what you will let into your head and your heart, and what you will and will not believe. Only you know your own truth. Negative people and influences are everywhere, but with the right protection, they won't be able to break through your barriers.

No matter how great our own day is going, we sometimes wander into someone else's negativity and bad manners. For instance, someone cuts in front of us in line or another person is in a bad mood and takes it out on us by being nasty and rude. These situations have nothing to do with us, but nevertheless, we soak up the negativity like a sponge. As a result, our day becomes less happy and less productive. Don't let anyone or anything steal your joy. Remind yourself that it is their problem and not yours, and try to forgive their rudeness. Keeping this rule in mind will lighten your mood again and you can continue to experience the great day you deserve!

Every day we hear mixed messages, both positive and negative, from those around us. If those negative messages, however minor, are allowed to sink in and take root, your mind power will be weakened. That's why it's so important to gain control over your thoughts so that when negative roadblocks are thrown at you, you can counteract or overcome them.

Other people's reactions and opinions are simply that—other people's reactions and opinions. They're based on their experience, and usually none of it has anything to do with you. It doesn't make you wrong, guilty, bad or unworthy. If someone is able to push your buttons, they've simply touched a place in you where there's an emotional wound. Next time someone gets that reaction from you, use your feelings to become aware of the wound. Then realize that all wounds eventually heal.

The more successful you become, the more you may notice that others will try to bring you down. It's a matter of weeding out the naysayers. You are the only one with the power to accept or reject what others say about you. The only opinion that really counts is *yours*!

People who hurt you or try to bring you down often have problems of their own. They feel the need, usually because of their own low self-esteem, to make you feel small. This helps them deflect their own thoughts of inadequacy. Let it go. I like to imagine myself wearing an invisible shield that protects me every time a negative comment or hurtful dart comes my way. Try it . . . it works!

I like to tell the story about some men that were running a race. They were all a little overweight. During the race, the people on the sidelines were remarking, "They'll never make the finish line! They're all too fat!" One by one, each man dropped to the ground, panting and gasping for breath. There was only one that ran through the finish line, and he was the heaviest of all. Why did he keep going while the others dropped out? Because he was DEAF!! Because he couldn't hear the naysayers, he persevered and wasn't discouraged. Make that a mantra for your life. Be deaf when others tell you it's impossible.

It's hard, believe me! I used to be like a rollercoaster ride. If someone complimented me, I'd soar high on that all day. But, on the other hand, if someone that same day seemed unimpressed, I'd be scraping the ground wondering what I did wrong. It's all so subjective. The truth is, if we depend on others for our self-esteem, we will never, ever be happy or content. We must, instead, learn to listen to and love ourselves—flaws and all!

Complain, complain, complain

Turn complaints into positives. Whenever you find yourself complaining, add a "but" and a new statement to turn it into a positive. For example, "I hate doing housework! But I am burning calories every time I bend down to pick something up." Use complaints to identify your likes as well as your dislikes.

No matter how beautiful the day is, there are always people who don't realize it because they are focusing on the less favorable elements of the day instead of being grateful for the blessings in front of them. Having a beautiful day means not only enjoying the weather, but exercising gratitude and recognizing all the privileges afforded you. It's about looking past the negatives so that we can enjoy these beautiful days more often. We can't always control the weather, but we can have a beautiful day every day. It's our choice!

I recently spent time with someone who is going through a divorce. All she kept saying was how much she regretted that she ever married this man and wasted ten years of her life with him. I told her that nothing in life is a waste; regretting things you've done in the past is a waste of energy. I suggested she forgive herself, forgive him, and move on. Regrets weigh us down and paralyze us from moving forward. Everything in life, whether good or bad, is a valuable experience. You may not see it at the time, but the knowledge gained reveals itself later on. Every negative experience can be turned into a positive experience.

Two people have the same Monday morning scenario: They both have to get up early, they have to sit in rush hour traffic, then get to a job that they may or may not like. One will complain and moan about her fate in life; the other will be grateful just to be alive and able to have the opportunity to get to a job. We create the conditions in our lives, positive or negative, healthy or unhealthy. Even though both are in the same position, the second person will ultimately see a better result with life than the first. Why? Because attitude determines the outcome of your life! Don't get me wrong. A positive attitude alone will not make all your dreams come true. But, with that great attitude comes a better chance of reaching any goal you envision. So, as you make your way toward your destination today, make sure you stay on track with the right attitude because it will turn your life around

You lose friends and blame it on the fact that someone must be saying bad things about you. You don't look where you're walking, stub your toe, and kick the dog. You oversleep and are late for work, so you blame in on traffic. Don't blame others for your lot in life. Learn from your mistakes. Take control of your life by admitting your faults. This is a powerful step in the right direction. Many people make excuses for their behavior. They blame everyone and everything except themselves. As Dwight Eisenhower said, "The search for a scapegoat is the easiest of all hunting expeditions."

One night we were dining at a restaurant when two elderly couples sat down at the next table. We couldn't help but hear their conversation for the first few minutes. "The economy is terrible," "doctors and dentists are all thieves," "this weather is the worst." The central topic of their dinner was complaining. Fortunately, we were finishing our meal when they arrived, so we were able to walk away from their negativity. If we had stayed and heard more complaints, we too would have started feeling negative and depressed about our lives. Negativity is around us all the time, invading our space like ants at a picnic. Stop listening.

A great thing to do after listening to a negative person complain is to ask him to now tell you something positive. If you ask this each time he says something negative, you may get through to him just how much negative energy he's projecting. Or the thought may make him realize that he doesn't like what he's doing. Or he may decide it's not worth complaining to you because he knows you'll ask him to think of something positive afterward.

For many of us, complaining has become such a habit that it becomes second nature to think in negative terms. We complain about the rain, we complain about the cold, we complain that it's too hot. Does complaining ever solve anything? No. All it does is make our world more negative. Ponder these thoughts:

1. Why do we complain about our jobs when thousands are out of work?

2. Why do we complain we have to exercise when many can't even walk?

3. Why is it that we complain that our house is too small when many are homeless?

The list can go on and on.

By complaining about your situation in life, you are trashing all the bountiful blessings you have been given. Stay grateful for what you *do* have instead of what you don't. When you find yourself beginning to complain, think back at my list and say, "why am I complaining about _____ when _____?"

Coping with bullies

Stop bullying. No one deserves to feel worthless.
—Rebecca Black

I've been actually really very pleased to see how much awareness was raised around bullying and how deeply it affects everyone. You know, you don't have to be the loser kid in high school to be bullied. Bullying and being picked on comes in so many different forms.
—Lady Gaga

Recently, while stopped in traffic, I noticed a bunch of children, not more than 11 or 12 years old, walking down the street laughing hysterically after being dropped off by the school bus. A few yards ahead of them was a boy about the same age. He was walking with his head down, seemingly agitated. The boy was overweight and it was then that I realized that the reason for the laughter was that one child was screaming insults at him, much to the amusement of the others.

There are a few things that ignite a strong reaction from me, and one of them is when I see someone being bullied. Maybe it's because I myself was the target of mocking laughter when I was that age. Maybe it's because my son, at the very same age, was tormented relentlessly for having bright red hair and freckles and being a little overweight. Maybe I should have minded my own business, but isn't that what most people do? Maybe I should have driven on and convinced myself that they will eventually leave this poor kid alone, but isn't that what most people do? I followed my gut and pulled over to the curb, rolled down my window, and gave them a piece of my mind. I told them to put themselves in his shoes. How would they feel if the shoe was on the other foot? How would they feel if I started laughing at a perceived flaw that I saw in each and every one of them? Does it make them feel powerful to belittle another human being? After speaking my mind, I expected the inevitable backtalk. Much to my surprise, some seemed embarrassed. The kid who initiated the laughter with his words, however, stood there in defiance. As I drove away and looked in my rear view mirror, he continued laughing, probably now at me! But what I also noticed was that the others were no longer laughing. Had I made an impact? I don't know. I do know that the bully will need a lot more discouragement from others in order to stop. His habit is too ingrained for one person's reaction to change it.

Let me tell you what my son had to endure. We live on a cul-de-sac; in two houses across from us lived some boys who were the best of friends. They were a year or two older than my son, and as soon as we moved in, the abuse started. My son would be in our driveway playing by himself when they, for no reason, would start throwing rocks at him. I scolded them but the same thing would happen on a daily basis. As soon as I stepped out the door, they would run away. It got to the point where my poor son was afraid to go out. Then came the time for him to start school. At the bus stop, the abuse was relentless. They would make believe they were his friend and ask him if they could see his book bag. Since my son was trying so hard to please them, he would hand it to them in hopes that maybe now they really would be his friend. Of course, once they got the bag, they threw it as far as they could, causing laughter and high fives. I had finally had enough of trying to reason with these boys and decided to talk to the parents. Two of the boys lived with their single father and a nanny. The father was working most of the time, so I had to talk to the 19-year-old nanny. She was trying her best to handle these kids, but she wasn't able to reel them in. I then moved on to the home of the third boy. My expectation was that the mother of this boy would agree that this was unacceptable behavior and offer to take action with her son and possibly even punish him for his behavior. Boy, was I shocked! Instead of listening to my polite pleas for her son to stop tormenting my son, she started screaming at me! How dare I complain about her son. He is an angel and does well in school!! Who was I to come to her door and complain? Well, there it was in a nutshell. I now realized why her son behaved the way he did. He could do no wrong and never had to face the consequences for bad behavior.

It was then that I decided I had to take a different approach. Since the bullying was occurring at the school bus pickup and drop-off area, I realized that it was now a school issue. I made a complaint to the school. The boys were called down to the principal's office and given a talking-to. That evening, the same mother who got angry with me, along with her husband, came banging at our door and made all kinds of threats against us. How dare I go to the school and make a complaint, they screamed. (Notice how the bullying is evident in the parents as well as their son.) I told them I had no choice. Our quality of life is just as important as theirs, and because of their son, ours was awful. If they had dealt with their son's bad behavior, I wouldn't have taken the issue to the school.

From that day on, these kids never even looked at my son. Eventually both houses were sold and they moved away. But what they did to my son will never be fully erased. My son is now in his late 20s, and the experiences he tolerated as a child have probably shaped what he has become as an adult. Thank goodness, his bad childhood experience with bullying hasn't kept him from being a successful businessman.

The experience of being bullied, whether it is verbal, physical, cyber-related or just being excluded from a group, is a universal epidemic. It's nothing new. It's not something that has just arisen in this generation, but it is a very hot topic. Tune into any talk show and there will be a celebrity talking about being bullied as a child. Unfortunately, even though there are more and more prevention programs in the schools, I believe that bullying is something that will never entirely go away. As long as there are humans, there will be those who get pleasure in making others feel small.

There is no sugar-coated way to put this: Bullying is ABUSE. Abuse of another person is a selfish, narcissistic and sadistic act perpetrated on victims who do not deserve to be treated in this way. The emotional and physical well-being of their victim is less important than their thrill of gaining dominance over the victim and attention from others. Bullying causes long-term emotional damage. You don't have to be physically bullied, as words and gestures do just as much harm. The old saying, "Sticks and stones may break my bones, but words can never harm me," seems wrong to me. Broken bones can mend. A black eye heals. What is more difficult to mend is the worst wound of all: Damage to a victim's self-identity. Bullies want to instill fear and self-loathing, and they usually are successful. No one deserves to feel undesirable, incapable and ineffective as an individual, but that is what happens at the hands of a bully. Being bullied at a young age makes you feel unsafe in a world where you should always feel safe. It causes depression, anger and bitterness. Eventually, you begin to believe the label the bully has placed on you. Unfortunately, our identity arises from social interactions starting in childhood. We start off as clay waiting to be molded. Our self-confidence is continually shaped by those around us, whether it's overt or subtle. That is why many people who were bullied as children follow a group mentality as adults. They want to feel that they belong to something, something they never were allowed to belong to as children because they were considered outcasts.

There are many bad short-term effects of bullying, but I think the long-term effects are scarier. Kids who were bullied are likely to have some serious long-term impacts. They're more likely to bully others and less likely to be offered job opportunities. They have lingering feelings of anger and bitterness, difficulty trusting others, and show fear and avoidance of social situations. They're also overly sensitive and thin-skinned and have a severe lack of self-esteem.

Bullying victims need support. We cannot be innocent bystanders. My son always knew that he had a healthy family support system to compensate for the bullying. My husband and I always made it clear to him that he is smart, talented and handsome. There is nothing we can do to prevent people from being nasty to us or our children. But we can make sure we fill our kids' heads with a lot of positive feedback so that those words will ring in their ears when the negative comments arise. I also make it a point to compliment someone who, to me, looks like he or she is low in self-confidence. While standing on line in a store one day, I noticed a young girl with her mom. Her posture was terrible—a first clue to a person's self-esteem. I told her that she had beautiful hair and, like magic, she straightened up and beamed with happiness. It doesn't take much. If we all as human beings decided to say something nice to someone on a daily basis instead of belittling, smirking or poking fun, maybe then the bullies in this world will take a lesson.

We must teach our children at the earliest age possible that it is *not* okay to hurt the feelings of others because they look different, have different beliefs or don't enjoy the same activities as you. Realize that if we want the world to be at peace, we must start in our own backyards!

I grew up being bullied about my freckles and short curly hair. The words cut like a knife and I wanted to crawl into a hole. Later on, I too became a bully. To myself! I started using the same words as those who bullied me: "Your freckles are ugly," "Ugh, look at your hair!" The hurt felt the same. That's what a bully wants. Bullies want you to feel lousy because it gives them a power they don't own. Negative self-talk is in internal form of bullying. Constantly telling yourself how bad you are and how you will never be a winner is your inner bully talking. Take away that power! Just as you would do with a schoolyard bully, stand up for yourself and say "I won't be bullied!"

Fill in the blank: "The thing I appreciate about myself at this very moment is_____." Focus on that and let's eradicate bullying!

Jealousy

Don't confuse having less with being less, or having more with being more, or what you have with who you really are.
—Noah benShea

We all sometimes look at someone else and wish we had her nose or his hair, her height or his build, etc. Did you know that there are six billion people on this planet—and no one is exactly the same! That means there's only one of you in this world. And you owe it to yourself to be the best you that you can possibly be! So don't waste a second of your time wishing you were someone else. You are unique, and uniqueness is a valuable asset!

Life is not a scoreboard at a football game. It's not about how many people return your calls or how many party invitations you receive. It's not about your hair or your shoes, where you live or what college you attended. It isn't about how accepted you are. It's just not about that. Life is about who you are kind to and who you hurt. It's also about how you feel about yourself. It's about trust, goodness and compassion. Life is about avoiding jealousy, overcoming obstacles and building confidence. It's about saying what you mean and meaning what you say. It's about seeing people for who they are and not what they have. Most of all, it's about your choice to touch the life of someone else in a most positive way. That's what life is all about.

When you are jealous of others

Do you ever resent someone else because he or she is in a place or position where you'd like to be? Use that feeling to become inspired to reach the same heights. Realize that the reason most people are enviously thin or impressively successful at their job is because of their tenacity and hard work! Nothing comes easy, and often the most successful people are the ones who just never give up, no matter what!

When we see others achieving more than we have achieved, or having more than we have, we get jealous and resentful. This reaction is destructive and only wastes the energy we could be using toward our own greatness. Use others' success as inspiration instead of jealousy. Follow their examples and make note of what they have done to achieve their success. Here's a metaphor for jealousy and success. If you put one crab in a bucket, it will eventually find a way to climb out. But if you put a bunch of crabs in a bucket, none will ever escape because as soon as one crab reaches the top, the others reach up, grab onto it, and pull it back. Now, crabs don't really think about why they do this, but it is a perfect metaphor for human behavior. All too often, when we see another person getting ahead or reaching success, we try to pull them down. Let's not be crabs. Let's support each other, be proud of each other, and be thankful instead of jealous!

When we feel a lack of something in our life, we tend to compare ourselves to others who we think have it better. This constant comparison and envy is a surefire way to derail your self-confidence train. You are on a journey in this life . . . not a competition. Follow each path of your journey via your own road map and not someone else's. If you must make a comparison, compete against yourself. Compare who you were a few months ago to who you are today. What have you learned, how much have you grown and what positive steps have you taken to reach your goals? Comparing ourselves to others is another habit that *can* be broken. Honor your own mix of talents and great qualities—this is what makes *you* special!

As much as some would love you to believe it, no one has a perfect life. In this age of Facebook and Twitter, depending on who you follow and what you read, you may think that everyone is successful and stress-free except you. Some would have you believe that they run a successful business with never-ending clients. Others would have you believe that they never have to diet to look the way they do. Realize that it's very easy, especially on the Internet, to inflate the truth with no consequences. No one wants to reveal the flaws and imperfections in their life. Some use Facebook to convince themselves that their fantasy is truth. Bottom line: Few will admit their life isn't perfect, so don't look to others with envy. Concentrate on your own accomplishments. Look back at the past few months and give yourself credit for even the smallest achievements. Life is not about viewing photos and status updates from others and feeling jealous. That's not reality. Live your authentic life, live your own truth, and don't believe the hype!

I do think if there's someone you look up to as a role model, it's good to try to emulate what he or she does—but only to the point of making yourself a better *you*, not a carbon copy of someone else. We often measure our success by comparing ourselves to others. Instead, we should strive for personal excellence, which is all about doing our best and maximizing our gifts, talents and abilities to perform at our highest potential. Our personal best is not about winning the game; it's about playing the game to the best of our ability. Or as Omer B. Washington wrote, "I've learned you shouldn't compare yourself to the best others can do, but to the best you can do."

We often are quick to forget the compliments or positive reinforcements that we receive from others. Don't focus on your loss if someone else gets a big break. Instead, remember the time you got praised, promoted or nabbed a client. Recognize your successes and celebrate them. It's only a matter of time until your next big break.

Malcolm Forbes once said, "Diamonds are nothing more than chunks of coal that stuck to their jobs." Coal starts off ugly and dirty and then, under incredible pressure, is turned into one of the earth's most precious and beautiful possessions. If jealousy and resentment are making you feel pressured to give up and quit, instead get tenacious! See that pressure as the very thing that will make your life the beautiful result that you desire it to be. Turn your jealousy into admiration, and that feeling of pressure into tenacity toward reaching your goals, and you will learn, grow and be transformed.

When others are jealous of you

When I was around 10 years old, I got a new sweater that I loved. I ran down the stairs in my apartment building to my best friend on the fourth floor to show her. She said it was nice, but that she was also going to get a new sweater, in a nicer color. I didn't think much of her comment at the time, but later that day after we played our usual games, when I went to pick up my sweater to go home, I noticed a little hole that wasn't there when I arrived. I was so upset, I ran upstairs crying. It wasn't until I became a little older that I realized my friend, out of jealousy, created that hole while I was in the bathroom (she later admitted it). She was resentful because I had something she didn't. She became angry and acted on her temporary thoughts of hatred by taking away what I had.

Jealousy is an unfortunate aspect of human behavior, and something we all have to deal with at some point. But it's harder to take when it's directed at you from someone who's supposed to be a friend.

Responding to jealous people takes lots of patience and a strong sense of self. It may help if you can understand that jealousy is a characteristic of insecure people suffering from very low self-esteem. When they perceive someone else as being successful in ways that they are not, they cover up their feelings with negativity and overly critical or sarcastic remarks.

So how do you interact with someone you know is jealous of you? Try complimenting him or her. By doing that, you diminish some of the jealousy by making the person feel more secure. Jealous people feel as though they lack the things they perceive others to have. They need to be reassured that they're just as worthy as those around them. We all need reassurance; jealous people simply need it more often!

If that doesn't work, simply avoid them for a little while. Or, if they're downright mean, avoid them completely. Most of the time, compassion and knowing the "why" behind a jealous person's behavior can really make the difference in changing the way that person reacts toward you. She may still have personal issues to deal with, but that doesn't have to stop you from choosing to look beyond the jealousy and into her heart.

We should be proud of others' successes as well as our own. We're all successful in our own way. We just have to focus on what's good in our lives and not what's missing. As Ken Keyes, Jr. aptly put it, "To be upset over what you don't have is to waste what you do have."

2

Creating Peace Within

I originally entitled this chapter "Finding Peace Within" but quickly realized that wasn't right. "Finding" implies that peace is something you search for, something you may or may not ever locate. "Creating" is more appropriate, because peace can be envisioned, defined and worked toward. You really can create peace in your life.

What Does Peace Represent to You?

To me, inner peace is a combination of happiness, well-being and balance: a feeling of wholeness and the notion that all is going our way. When you feel this way, it makes getting along with others easy.

Think of peace, happiness and well-being as your natural state, as who you are. It doesn't come from material things. It's an inside job.

The first step in creating peace is identifying what it means to you. How would you define happiness for you? What is your personal vision of well-being? What does peace look like to you, and how does it feel?

Write it down. Allow yourself to feel your responses, your memories of times you've felt whole and calm and happy. What about those times contributed to those great feelings?

Now that you've defined it, what can you do to manifest it in your life?

Consciously choose happiness

Happiness is not something we must earn, the way we have to earn a living. It really is our choice. And no one can tell you that you can't be happy, no matter your circumstances.

That sense of well-being and satisfaction with your life comes from a combination of two things: fun without meaning (think massages) and meaning without fun (like waking up with your baby in the middle of the night). Having consistent fun without meaning will make you feel empty inside. But, on the other hand, if you focus only on obligations, you'll end up tired and resentful. Happiness requires a balance: You have to incorporate a little of both into your routine.

Our natural instinct is to be happy, but as time passes and life's experiences unfold, we sometimes lose our spirit. When that happens, we lose our perspective and can fall into a habit of negative thinking. No matter what has happened to take away your smile, you can choose to find it again. Here are some ideas:

Stand in front of a mirror, look into your eyes and smile. Tell yourself how wonderful you are and that you deserve to be happy. Do this a few times a day, even if it feels silly. This will work wonders to lift your spirits!

Be grateful. In a study done in Japan, happy and unhappy participants felt the same number of negative moments each day. The only difference: The happy and content ones had more frequent positive moments. Try to recognize good things when they happen, to you and to others. Keep a journal and write down all the things you have to be grateful for. You can't be grateful and grumpy at the same time!

If we were able to go back in time and fix every negative experience that happened to us, life would be meaningless. Even if it's hard to accept, we can't change the past. But we do have the power to change the future as a result of the mistakes we made in the past—and that's a beautiful lesson. We all make mistakes, but as long as you let the past go, your future can be bright, knowing that things were meant to happen. The rope of life is complex but solid. Trust its strength and hold on for the greatest climb ever!

If you are in a bad mood, lose yourself for a little while. Find something to do that requires effortless concentration. Some people take a boat out on the ocean; I do crossword puzzles. Whatever activity energizes you and makes the time go by will bring back your flow.

Recognize that you can't buy your way to happiness. Don't get me wrong, money is great to have. It makes our lives easier in many ways. But a nationwide study published in *Social Indicators Research* in 2008 found that people who pursue possessions were less satisfied with friendships, families, jobs and even health than those who were less materialistic.

We may not want to admit it, but we're on a constant mission to impress others. Whether it's the kind of car we drive, the restaurants we frequent or the size of our house or boat, we want to impress others. These things may draw some attention to you, but it won't last for long. People with character realize that possessions aren't as impressive as qualities. How many people do you know who own impressive possessions but have no real values? Now imagine a person who has great integrity, cares about others and can hold a conversation without the word "I" in it. Would this person impress you? Would it matter if this person weren't rich? When someone tries to impress you or you try to impress others with possessions, realize that it's who you are and how you live your life that really is impressive.

Finding happiness within

Learn to look for happiness inside yourself, on your terms. If you seek it from outside yourself, your happiness will forever be at the mercy of forces you can't control. Rather than basing your happiness on inconstant things such as approval from others or having the right (fill in the blank: home, car, shoes, etc.), base it on what's inside of you—your inner strength, your unique personality, your sense of humor, your refusal to let your spirit be broken. If the source of your happiness is within you, steady like a pilot light, you'll be able to access it and seek its comfort anytime you want.

Don't try to be perfect. Of course, we want to do it all. A fast way to become unhappy is to try to juggle more than we can handle. Striving to be something that is unobtainable, like the perfect parent, wife or employee, will only make you feel inadequate. Decide to be happy despite your imperfections. Nobody's perfect, even though media images make us believe that. (I'll say more about dealing with perfectionism later in this chapter.)

Start the day by thinking about your accomplishments. You may think you've done nothing special, but did you raise a family? That's an accomplishment. Did you visit your parent or say a kind word to a friend? These are actions worthy of praise. If you think only of what you haven't done, you become sad and guilt-ridden. You can't change what's done, you can't control what's to come, but you can influence this present moment. Remember, a positive attitude has a huge influence on physical health. It makes you feel better, feeling better makes you happier, feeling happier brings more people and opportunities in your life, and so on. What a happy cycle!

Simply move! You can increase happiness just by involving your body. Dance around the house, jump rope, do some tummy crunches. Go out and take a walk in the park. All these things will rev you up, which in turn brings on a happy feeling.

Forgive as much as you can. It's hard to let go of anger and resentment toward others, especially if a person has hurt us deeply. Consider that anger is like a poison. It can raise blood pressure and cortisol levels. Is that person or situation really worth harming your health? Think of the circumstances surrounding the event that caused your hurt. Maybe that person was having a bad day. Many times, forgiving is really a gift to yourself. It can do more for you than for the person you are forgiving.

Whatever you do, don't give anyone the power to steal your joy. Your joy is what empowers you.

Helping others to be happy is the best way to ensure your own happiness. This can be as simple as offering a smile or as involved as volunteering with an organization to provide food or shelter to someone who needs it. Fixing our minds on something other than ourselves makes us feel capable, gives us perspective and keeps us from obsessing about ourselves for a while. And according to a 2006 article in *Proceedings of the National Academy of Sciences*, being charitable actually boosts blood flow to the part of the brain associated with reward. This doesn't mean you have to fill your schedule with community service. Just be kind. Give that homeless person on the corner a dollar. Hold a door for someone else. It's enough to boost your happiness level.

More than ever these days, people are stressed, uncertain, and most likely, depressed. In our hurried and seemingly impersonal society, the compliment you give to a stranger may be the only nice thing they will hear all day. You can't imagine how you can make someone's day with a simple nice word. A compliment generates mutual feelings of happiness between a giver and a receiver. Paying a sincere compliment actually makes you feel more attractive! It's a gift that costs nothing, yet can be the most rewarding gift you can give another human being. It can also benefit you! You cannot give a sincere compliment to another person without feeling great yourself—it's impossible. So, today make it a priority to make someone's day. Find something special and unique about them and let them know.

One of the keys to happiness is making the best out of every situation. When my dad lived alone in his 90s, he depended on me for many of his needs. On the two days he didn't get dialysis, I would do his grocery shopping and take him to doctor appointments. Instead of looking at it as a sad situation, I was fortunate to realize then that I needed to reframe my thoughts. I came to see these times with my dad as precious, fleeting chances to bond with him before he passed away. I also was happy to have the opportunity to give back to him a little of what he did for me as a child. Reframing our thoughts can become a habit. Even if you have to fake it at first—smile when you feel like crying—you will learn to engage your thoughts in a way that produces happiness.

We go to Broadway theaters often, and that includes parking our car in the theater district with all the crowds of people doing the same. It's not the best part of the experience, but sometimes it's actually a pleasure. Recently, an extremely jovial and witty man welcomed us into the lot with a friendly, "Hello, and welcome!" After that, the attendant who gave us the ticket for our car kindly opened the door for me and helped me out, all the while smiling and making jokes. He wished us a great evening and even told us not to forget our umbrella in case it rains. At another parking lot I use often, the attendant tells me how much he's missed me whenever I return to his establishment. He always has my car waiting for me when I return. These cheerful, helpful people always make me realize that every single job, even those we sometimes look down on as menial, is important. No matter what you do, you make someone's day brighter if you have the best attitude and project that attitude onto others. A CEO would be nothing without his secretary, a dentist couldn't practice his craft without a dental assistant. So, if you think what you do for a living isn't important, I hope you will change your mind. Don't just go through the motions, be the best you can be. You would be surprised how your little job has a huge impact on those who count on you.

SUE SAYS
Happiness is a state of mind—not a state of affairs.

Do something you love—often
We are more stressed out, burned out and tapped out today than ever before, and that is why it is important to pursue activities or hobbies that relieve stress and bring us joy. A great hobby will keep you focused on the present—not sad about the past or worrying about the future.

Cooking, gardening, photography, painting—what activities fire your passions? What hobbies help you to lose sense of time because you're having so much fun? Personally, I love to play the piano, and when I sit down to play anything from the Beatles to Rodgers and Hammerstein, all my stress disappears! Another thing I love to do is dance. I put on a soundtrack of dance music, and the time seems to fly. Plus, I'm releasing those much needed exercise endorphins at the same time!

When I'm in the audience at an orchestra concert, I often wonder if the guy playing the triangle, or the fourth lady playing the viola, is really being heard. They may be playing instruments that aren't the loudest, yet they are just as important to the overall sound of the music as the drums or the trombone. It's the same with life. You may not think you matter or that you have anything to offer others, but you do! I may not be famed motivational speaker Tony Robbins, but I remind myself on a daily basis that even if the only thing I do today is offer a bit of encouragement or motivation to another person, that's perfect! And, even if someone doesn't like what I have to say, I am content knowing that at least I offered it.

Do the things that relax you. Some people find that just going for a walk in the park is enough to feel more relaxed. Others enjoy baking, scrapbooking or crafting. (Creating something fabulous makes you feel good about yourself, which is an added benefit!)

Whatever this activity is for you, try to do it as much as possible.

Enjoy the simple things in life

> *Enjoy the little things, for one day you may look back and realize they were the big things.*
>
> —Robert Brault

It's wonderful to have big goals and plans for the future. Looking forward to that fancy car or vacation home is great, but the everyday, smaller and simpler pleasures can bring you as much fulfillment as the larger, more expensive things. You just have to pay more attention.

Keep working toward your goals, but also take time to recognize the things going on in your life that bring you happiness right now. Find your little, simple pleasures and sprinkle them throughout your day.

To give you an idea of what I mean, here are the personal pleasures that make my day. These aren't big things, no drum roll is required. But they are things I look forward to each and every day. Many are free or cost next to nothing. Here goes:

When I open my eyes in the morning, I can't wait to have my favorite blueberry muffins and a hot cup of coffee. Along with my breakfast, watching the news while reading one of my favorite magazines is, to me, the start of a wonderful day.

Sitting in my beautiful, airy kitchen early in the morning, I love watching the sun come up gradually. Nature at its best!

I love dancing on my trampoline, boxing and doing my rowing machine. You may think I'm crazy, but doing this every day has become a comforting ritual. When I'm away from home, I feel a void. I miss my routine.

I love coming into my kitchen after my workout and enjoying turkey, spinach, berries and my daily portion of dark chocolate.

I love my Red Zinger tea (I prepare it with a splash of pomegranate extract).

I love writing my daily blog tips on my Facebook page. When someone makes a positive comment, it really makes my day!

I love relaxing in a hot bath.

I love eating my daily sesame bagel (just the outside).

I love listening to Sinatra and Broadway tunes on Sirius radio as I drive.

I love hearing the sound of my sons playing guitar.

I love when my husband calls periodically during the day to see how I am.

I love meeting people throughout the day and learning about them.

I love my carrots and sunflower seeds.

I love my daily glass of wine.

I love a crisp, tart apple!

I love Manhattan.

I love visiting my family in upstate New York at their 18th-century stone house.

I love visiting my family in Montreal.

I love licorice (but only black).

I love a good true crime book or biography.

I love sitting in my massage chair.

I love the smell of the air right before the rain.

I love freshly fallen snow.

And I love making people smile.

Pretty great stuff, huh? These are some of my simple pleasures. Now, come up with a list of your own. Feel free to borrow and modify any of the ideas on my list. You'd be surprised how these little things that happen on a daily basis have the power to enrich our lives.

Learn to work with time and make it work for you

One of the simplest changes you can make to create peace is to slow down. Just slow down. Even if you are running late, don't allow yourself to become tense and rushed. Inhale slowly and exhale calmly.

The corollary to this is to stop over-scheduling yourself. Don't try to do and be everything in one day. Be realistic about what you can accomplish, and when. And build extra time into your schedule just for you.

Streamline your life. Are you flying on autopilot as you fulfill a full slate of activities and obligations? Are all of those activities really serving you and your family? Are your obligations truly that? Every so often, stop and take stock of what you're doing. You may find that some things are no longer worth your valuable time.

For those things you must or want to continue to do, is there a way to do them faster or more easily? A client of mine with a busy, deadline-intensive advertising job also loved acting and tried to perform with her favorite community theater at least three or four times a year. Rehearsals for these productions were a major commitment—up to four hours a night, five nights a week. When she was younger, this grueling schedule would put her home life in chaos; there was simply no time or energy left during the workweek to clean or put things in order. And she needed the weekends to rest and to be with her family. But along the way, she figured out things she could do just for the rehearsal and run of show to keep her home in order and herself sane. She hired a maid service to clean every other week for six weeks. She fed her six cats on paper bowls to cut down on dishwashing. As bills arrived through the mail, she stashed them in a zippered folder along with her checkbook and paid them during her downtime backstage. (This was before online banking made this process even easier.) She recorded her lines and listened to them during her work commute and while exercising, rather than spending her precious weekend time with a script in hand. The point is, streamlining your life isn't always about giving up activities. Sometimes it's about finding extra time within the activities you're already doing.

Before you go to sleep each night, prepare for the following day by writing down a To Do list. Once you've thought about everything you have to do and get it on paper, forget about it and go to sleep. This will help you avoid the endless tossing and turning that often occurs when you are unable to stop thinking about what needs to be done and what was forgotten the day before. Trust me—this one I know from experience!

However you choose to spend your time, remember not to give all of it, nor all of your energy, to the small stuff of life. Keep room in your days for the things that are truly important. Pay attention to the things critical to your happiness. Play with your children. Dance with your partner. Spend time with your parents and grandparents. There will always be time to close that deal, clean the house or paint the fence. First, take care of the things that truly matter. Set your priorities.

SUE SAYS

Devote a large portion of your time to things you do well. Don't overload yourself with too many challenges at once. Orchestrate your life so that you always have something to look forward to, and don't wait to pat yourself on the back. Give yourself credit for each iota of success.

Take Very, Very Good Care of Yourself

I bet most of you make sure your cell phone battery is consistently charged. But do you make sure *you* are recharged as needed? We can't think clearly or perform well when we keep running down our internal batteries. But once they are recharged, it's amazing how everything else seems to fall into place.

To achieve real happiness and satisfaction, make yourself your main priority. This isn't being selfish. A happy, successful and satisfied child, husband, friend or any other relationship in your life cannot occur without a happy, successful and satisfied *you!*

When our lives are filled with constant change, it's very difficult to remember to be compassionate with our bodies. We get caught up in the daily grind and forget our own basic needs: restful sleep, nourishing food, proper hydration, break activities that take our minds off what's bothering us, loving interaction with others.

Neglecting our bodies can simply make us feel tired and not at our best. But add stress, upset and negative feelings to the mix, and you may also experience tight shoulders, stomach cramps, a stiff neck or a headache.

It is an absolute *must* to make yourself and your needs a priority. There's a reason we're instructed on airlines to put the oxygen mask on ourselves first, then on our child or partner. If we don't help ourselves, we can't be any good to others. Be who you are. Don't assume that you always have to fit in or that you must conform to be liked and respected by others or face exclusion. Give yourself a break. Being a false version of yourself, and putting the expectation of others first is a huge burden to place on your unique self.

Stress is an inevitable part of life, but we can control its impact—and we can even have fun doing so. Here are some proven stress relievers:

Confide in someone you love and trust. Dance. Have fun with friends. Watch a funny movie or try laughter yoga! Get lost in a good book. Pray and hand your worries over to a higher power. Hang around positive people. Avoid negative influences. Take time off. Try an herbal solution such as Rescue Remedy (found in most natural food stores). Pursue a hobby. Work out regularly. Get a massage. Sit in a sauna or steam room. Do a little spring cleaning—any time of the year. Sing. Meditate. Take steps to change what's bothering you. Prune your to-do list. Look for the silver lining. Get enough sleep (seven to nine hours a night. Do it!). Smile. Work with passion. Accept what you can't change.

Breathe deeply, which is something most adults don't know how to do correctly. Breathing from the abdomen allows more oxygen to enter your system, which stimulates a relaxation response. (A great tip for lowering blood pressure is to pinch one nostril as you inhale, and then switch and pinch the other nostril as you exhale.)

Eat well. A balanced, nutritious diet of healthy proteins, vegetables and fresh fruit at regular intervals during the day will keep your blood sugar levels stable. Drink plenty of water. And limit caffeine and sweetened drinks, even the sugar-free kind.

Deal with the energy sappers in your life—the things you've procrastinated about doing but that stay on your mind. Do them or hire someone to do them for you. Get them off your plate!

Talk it out. Make sure you have someone who can listen to your problems: a friend, family member, life coach (like me!) or therapist. You can also keep a journal. Just don't self-medicate with food, shopping, too much internet surfing, and other distractions to numb or forget what is really bothering you.

And never forget to play! Some people may perceive playtime as silly, but they're missing the point. You need occasional periods of recreation in order to avoid burnout and to keep enjoying what you're doing with your life. Slow down and smell the roses! Play is more than something extra—it's a fundamental part of your life.

If times are very tough for you right now—say, you're grieving a job loss or the end of a relationship—just take small steps, but do take *some* steps to take care of yourself. The future will improve; it simply takes time. Focus on the big picture, and when you feel yourself sinking into despondent thoughts, realize it and move your attention to what's good and going right. Don't beat yourself up if things go completely wrong today. Remember, tomorrow is a new day and, with a positive attitude, it WILL be better.

Making time to be alone for some introspection and self-reflection can be an enlightening and empowering experience. It is during these moments that you will gain helpful insights for living. These insights can refine, reinforce or question your personal values and beliefs. Spending time alone isn't a punishment and doesn't suggest you're antisocial. It's great to be social, but having no expectations from anyone once in a while is great and can only lead to greater self-discovery. Once you gain more understanding of yourself, you can begin to appreciate and love all the talents and positive traits that are within you. Devoting time and energy to our well-being on a regular basis helps us to be more positive, more productive, more resilient, more loving toward others and more accepting of our own lives. Make this investment in yourself!

Develop a resilient spirit

Someone told me years ago, "Life is not about how fast you run, or how high you climb, but how well you bounce." It's true. We often don't have a choice in what happens to us, but we always have a choice in how we react. The key is building resilience, which will help you recover from any letdown.

My favorite metaphor for resilience is the bamboo tree. It can withstand gale force winds, bending to the ground and lifting back up again. It bends, but it doesn't break. When life becomes stormy for us, when it throws us constant curve balls, when it becomes so noisy that it's hard to maintain our happiness, that's when we need to bend like the bamboo tree—so we can lift back up again.

If you believe self-criticism is protecting you from unhappiness, think again. Research shows that people who beat themselves up have more depression and anxiety, are more self-indulgent and have a diminished sense of well-being. It's clearly in your best interest to stop the self-torture. Flaws and mistakes are a part of life, and resiliency is a necessary trait of all leaders.

Resilience keeps you feeling positive and strong. It lets you shake off that rude comment or rejection. It helps you pick yourself up when you inevitably stumble. It discourages you from giving up when what you need is to keep going.

Whenever we have to make a choice, whether it's changing jobs or buying a car, we can make long lists of the pros and cons and worrying about whether we're making a big mistake by going with the "wrong" choice. We can ponder the what ifs so much that it keeps us from moving forward. Forget about analyzing everything. These aren't life-and-death decisions. We can never have all the information nor predict the future. The world will not come to an end if you make a mistake, so don't limit yourself and sweat over choosing incorrectly. No matter what you choose in life, whether it turns out to be a right or wrong decision, you will gain growth and knowledge that can never be experienced if we are afraid of wrong decisions. You can handle whatever the outcome, because you are resilient. Remind yourself that whatever choice you make, it's the right choice.

Never let a crisis shake your spirit. Stay calm. No matter what happens, keep a good opinion of yourself. Play the reel of your past successes as the motion picture in your mind. No matter what you lose, no matter what failures you endure, keep faith in yourself. You can then stand up to any crisis with calm and courage, refusing to buckle.

Life can go from calm to chaotic in the blink of an eye. When a catastrophe strikes, it can send us into a complete panic. A riptide can strike a calm ocean in a split second, and if you're caught in it, the worst thing to do is panic and fight against it. The reason people don't survive a riptide is because they exhaust themselves trying to swim against this strong and powerful force. If they relax and float along with the current, eventually the waters calm again. The same goes for panic. Don't flail around and try to fight against what's going on. Stay calm and conserve your energy. You must know that, just like a riptide, your life will eventually settle down and calmness will prevail again.

You really *can* handle anything that life throws at you. You may not be able to handle it perfectly or expediently, but you will handle it. Sometimes life isn't the party we hoped for, but while we're here, we might as well dance!

Staying strong during periods of pain and suffering

Recently I went to the cemetery to visit my the graves of my parents. They died within two years of each other, and these visits are always difficult. Every time I go, I stand there and ponder how my mom and dad could possibly be there and not still with me. I still can't wrap my mind around it! These visits always leave me with a knot in my stomach for days after. One way I unravel the knot is to think of the musical numbers my dad played on the piano and performed in the theater; I also look around my home and see all the beautiful artwork my mom created. I thought of how many countries they traveled to and all the photographs they took along the way. I could go on and on, but, what I realize is, they did what they loved and lived a full, happy life. I hope that my children will think of their parents in the same way and realize this lesson: Life is so short. The past is gone and the future is here for us to create. The power is in this moment. In this moment, we have the choice to create painful memories from the past, or we can create a beautiful tomorrow. I try to celebrate my parents for how they lived and not mourn their deaths.

Every once in a while, life throws us into overwhelming situations with which we can't cope. It could be the death of a loved one, an illness or plain old depression. Anger and resentment can sometime be the byproducts of our pain. It seems everyone is sweet and charming when the skies are sunny and everything's going well. But, the true character of a person shines through by how they deal with hardship.

Do you believe your circumstances aren't your fault? There may be some degree of truth in this, but even so, blaming leaves you feeling powerless. Having a victim mentality steals the power you own and weakens you tremendously. Ultimately, you are the only person who has the ability to change your situation. When you begin to take responsibility, you feel better about yourself and more in control of your life. If you find yourself saying, "I can't help it," "It's their fault," "Things are just really hard for me," then it's time to change your self-talk to "It may be hard for me, but I will do everything in my power to change the situation."

For emotional pain and suffering, remember that everything is subject to change, including your situation. Be comforted in knowing that you are not alone. You don't have to feel isolated. There's a vast community of support groups with people going through the same thing you are. Reach out to others.

If you can't see the light at the end of the tunnel, push yourself to focus on the positive. One great thing to do is help others in the same situation. Contribute your time and energy. When we let a painful situation sink us into depression, we look at what we can't do and not what we can do. We begin to believe there's no other choice but to feel pain. We must allow the pain to leave us.

One of my favorite quotes is "Pain is inevitable, but suffering is optional." If you are in pain, I hope that whatever you are experiencing passes quickly. Like all things, suffering is not permanent!

Be your own best friend

Once, I received a phone call from a good friend who was feeling bad about herself and needed cheering up. Someone said something that hurt her ego, and with an already diminished self-image, this put her into a depression. Well, what are friends for? I reminded her of all her positive qualities and how talented and valuable she is.

Friends know what to say to cheer up a pal. They know when to offer a pep talk and when to sit back and listen. Usually, even if they disagree with something you're doing, they can be honest without being judgmental. They love you no matter what. They accept the way you look, your limitations and failures. They are there to help pick up the pieces and start again. Best friends never talk badly about you. They truly want the best for you!

So why not be your own best friend?

Best friends are respectful and hold each other in high esteem. They don't speak rudely to each other. When my friend started to doubt her capabilities, I jumped in and pointed out all her strengths, skills and past achievements. Friends are like coaches, encouraging you to reach your goals and dreams. What would your life be like if you did the same for yourself?

Most of us seek happiness outside ourselves: money, possessions, lovers. But you have to realize that there is no true contentment unless it comes from within. Many of us don't like what we see when we look too closely at ourselves. To be your own best friend, try to develop the same tolerance and loving attitude toward yourself as you would your dearest friend.

Choose to lift yourself up and not beat yourself down. It's entirely up to you. If you don't like something you're doing, change it. And if you can't change it, accept it with love and compassion. Stop beating yourself up. We all make mistakes. In fact, mistakes are the primary means of learning in life. Just tell yourself, "Next time, I'll try harder."

Pay attention to what you say to yourself. If you missed the alarm and overslept, instead of saying, "What an idiot, I'm going to be late now," replace it with "This was a good lesson for me. I'll set the alarm for an hour earlier tomorrow." Be careful, as negative self-talk is habit forming and adds to low self-esteem. Be kind and gracious to yourself.

Always give yourself the positive recognition you deserve when you do something you're proud of. Bask in your own glory . . . even if no one else notices. Don't wait for recognition from others. You'll only be disappointed if you don't get it. Complimenting ourselves and continual positive reinforcement stays with us like our own shadow.

Today, acknowledge that you are a splendid creation capable of the greatest accomplishments. You are one of a kind. Never before in the history of humanity and never again will there be another you. You have a purpose and a mission—and with that a responsibility to fulfill those goals. The key to success is in asserting and believing that you can, then purposefully taking action.

Compete with your personal best. If you've given 100 percent of your effort—whether it's in your professional life, your parenting or any other role—knowing that you've done your best or are willing to improve tomorrow is all you can ask of yourself.

Hold your own hand and be the most supportive person in your life. When you learn to be your own best friend, everything looks better, you become less dependent on others for your self-worth and you stop looking outside of yourself for happiness. By learning to respect yourself and realizing that you deserve only the best in life, you will earn the strength to go out and get it!

Embrace change

Clinging to what is comfortable is safe. We really are creatures of habit, and when a habit becomes comfortable we feel safe. It's easy to convince yourself that you should remain where you are because you have no place better to go. It's easy to allow things to eat away at your sense of self, your sense of value, your sense of well-being. It's easy to blame someone else and to ignore what you really feel. Eventually, you'll have to take the difficult step of taking responsibility for everything you experience and how you respond. Devote today to loving yourself, honoring yourself and removing yourself from negative and unloving thoughts.

In many instances, our comfort zones can also be the source of most of our problems. It is easy to maintain dysfunctional relationships or stay at a dead-end job. To improve your life, you will need to change your life: do new things, in new ways, with new people or in a new setting.

I recently had the honor of being the keynote speaker at an event. When I was first asked, my natural inclination was to say no. As a personal Life Coach, I'm not accustomed to motivational speaking. I decided to say yes anyway in order to challenge myself and break out of my comfort zone. Most of us stay in a comfort zone instead of taking the risk of failure. We stay safe that way, but we may never know what our true potential is and what we are capable of achieving. Stepping out of your comfort zone doesn't have to be something extraordinary—even a small step can be rewarding. For me, the indescribable feeling of accomplishment I got from the huge round of applause during and after my speech was validation that my courage paid off. Security doesn't come from outside ourselves . . . it lies within us!

Success requires risk on your part. The higher you reach, the less comfortable you'll feel. Letting go of your comfort zones may make you feel vulnerable, and the desire to hang on at any cost will be great. That's why change requires you to be both brave and bold. Everyone fears failure—but failure is nothing more than trying something and finding that it didn't quite work. There's always next time!

Think of personal change as improving and you'll realize that whoever you are now, you are slowly getting better and better. The way you are today is not a final state. Every day is an opportunity to grow in one way or another. Take one positive step toward improvement today and every day.

Ponder upon your future possibilities and that your potential is virtually unlimited. You can do whatever you want to do and go wherever you want to go. You can be the person you ultimately want to be. You can set large and small goals, make plans and move step-by-step, progressively toward their realization. There are no obstacles to what you can accomplish except the obstacles that you create in your mind.

What about changes outside of our control? We still control how we respond. We can choose to anticipate and embrace changes or resist them. Resisting change is like trying to push water upstream. Some people call change progress and celebrate it. Others curse those same changes and wish for the good old days. Same changes, different responses. Change is life. It's unavoidable, so work toward accepting it. Successfully dealing with change means choosing to grow. If you fail to grow, you fail to live fully.

Make a habit of letting go

When we travel, we try to take as little baggage as possible. So why do we hold on tight to the bags that weigh us down in our lives—bags of the past, of disappointment, of self-doubt, mistakes, fear, anger or pain? They only serve to slow us down and drain our energy.

To create peace, travel light in life. Put the bags away! Unburden yourself and the journey will be a lot more fun. The lighter the load, the easier to win the race.

When we clean out our closets, we feel a sense of lightness. The same is true for emotional, spiritual and psychological clutter. When we hold onto things—false beliefs, old insults, well-worn bad habits—they act as anchors to the past and weigh us down. Letting go allows us to begin something new and creates light and space that wasn't previously there.

When I want to cleanse my computer of some of the garbage I receive, I press "delete" and then "empty trash." When I find myself thinking a negative or self-defeating thought, I do the same . . . but in my mind. Even though I'm saying it to myself and not pressing a computer key, the effect is the same. By saying "delete," I remove the thought from my energy, and by "emptying" it, I permanently erase all traces of its existence in my thoughts. I then have a nice clean memory field to accept the thoughts I desire. So, the next time you receive a negative message, remember . . . DELETE and EMPTY TRASH!

Learn from your past, then put a period on it. Move forward from there and don't look back. If you are constantly looking back at your past, you are not moving forward!

Someone I worked with recently told me that she always had white knuckles from constantly having her hands clenched in anticipation of some horrible fate. Clenching her hands gave her an illusion of control. The truth is, the more you attempt to control things in your life, the more out of control you feel. Stop grasping so tightly and allow your life to flow naturally and easily. When you decide to loosen your death grip on control, that's when peace and happiness pour in. Believe that life is unfolding as it should, and replace the word "control" with the word "trust."

SUE SAYS

It isn't always enough to be forgiven by others. Sometimes you have to learn to forgive yourself.

Live a Life of Integrity

Integrity is, to me, the single most important character trait in a person. Keeping promises and doing what you say you will is perhaps the simplest and easiest way to build a strong character and develop high self-esteem. Developing a reputation for always coming through on your word will create more value in your life than you can ever imagine. You will be respected by your family, friends and business associates. If you earn a reputation for being trustworthy, your words and ideas will be more meaningful and valuable and you will see a marked improvement in many relationships. Once you believe in the importance and benefits of developing the highest level of integrity, your life will never be the same. Build your character by doing what you say and saying what you mean!

Integrity is a value that enhances every part of your life. It means being totally honest and truthful with yourself and with others. Keeping your word. Honoring your commitments. Like persistence, courtesy and courage, it's your choice whether to live by these values.

I do not believe integrity is something we're born with. You learn throughout the course of your life. It may be taught by our parents, since they are the first people who impact our life, but true integrity is something gained over time, regardless of what your upbringing was like. It comes from the relentless pursuit of honesty at all times. Nothing drains you more and causes more stress than knowing that you are not doing what is in alignment with your core values.

Integrity is the number-one quality of leaders. It's expressed in an absolute desire to keep one's word. The glue that holds life's relationships together is trust, and trust is based on integrity. When we seek to do business, we look for a company with a reputation for honesty and ethics. That's why we tend to shy away from business people we refer to as used-car salesmen. Somewhere down the road, they got a reputation for being dishonest and it stuck.

Promises are easy to make but often very hard to keep. Remember that every time you do what you say you are going to do, it's an act of integrity, which in turn strengthens your character. As you begin to act with integrity in everything you do, every part of your life will improve. Your confidence will grow. You will attract the best situations and people into your life. Those around you will notice. I believe one of our greatest personal assets is the way we are known and valued by our peers.

It's easy and comforting to blindly follow what others do and say without questioning their qualifications and without doing your own independent thinking and due process. It's harder to understand that people can be wrong than to do the necessary research into what they are telling you. Once upon a time, almost everyone believed the earth was flat. The few who went against the received wisdom, like Columbus, were first mocked, but then honored. Don't blindly follow others and don't adopt their opinions just because it's easier than thinking for yourself. Do your own research, be your own person, and use the intelligence you were born with. Stand by your own integrity.

Who you are, down to your core, is evidenced by what you do on a daily basis. Always do the right thing, even when no one is looking. Realize that what you do is your statement to the world, defining who you are. No matter how big a house you have or how slick a car you drive, the only thing you can take with you at the end of your life is your integrity. Be sincere and true to your word. Our words are a precious commodity and should be treated as such.

Most of us won't do huge heroic deeds that make headlines in the news. But by doing little things, we can all be heroic in life. We can be helpful, say kind words, face challenges with courage, stand up for what's right even when the cost is high, keep our word, and spread goodness instead of hate. This quiet heroism is the greatest heroism of all.

Remember the Law of Attraction! Be the person you want to attract in your life. And as Ralph Waldo Emerson said, "Guard your integrity as a sacred thing."

Fall in love with your wonderful self

Self-love is the foundation for all happiness. I truly believe if we don't respect and love ourselves, with all our imperfections, nothing else will ever make us content.

In the past, I spent lots of time demanding perfection of myself and, of course, falling short. Most people have a form of "I'm not good enough" that ruins their lives, work and relationships. Or they seek external validation of their worthiness: I'm only loveable and valuable if this important person thinks I am and tells me so.

Truth is, no one else can give us what only we can give ourselves. To be truly fulfilled, we must find the love within and give it to ourselves. No other person or possession can do it. It's up to us.

How would you feel if someone sent you encouraging and uplifting words every day? You'd know how much they cared, which would undoubtedly thrill you. Why not send yourself an e-mail every day extolling the virtues of you? Honor yourself . . . you deserve it! Send yourself an e-mail every day for at least 30 days with a new message of encouragement and love. Be your own biggest fan!

Your level of self-acceptance determines your level of happiness. They usually go hand in hand. The more self-acceptance you have, the more happiness you'll allow yourself to receive and enjoy. In other words, you enjoy as much happiness as you believe you're worthy of. Don't deprive yourself of this birthright. You can never find true happiness until you realize and become true to who you really are.

To love yourself is the greatest way to improve yourself, and as you improve yourself, you improve your world.

Use your experiences to gain perspective

Our perspective is everything when it comes to eliminating stress and being happy in our lives. Even when the glass appears to be half empty, our minds can find a way to see the glass as half full. When we trust that there is opportunity in every situation, our focus remains open and we don't let ourselves become victims.

Have you ever had something happen to you that seemed really bad at the time but later turned out to be beneficial? There are so many experiences where days, weeks, or even years later, we say, "That was the best thing that could have ever happened to me!" I have had many, many clients say that to me after a seemingly negative event touched their lives. Teach yourself the trick of finding the good in every situation and happiness will be your constant companion. You will save countless days and weeks of useless worry over situations that always work out to your benefit in the end!

We all have bad things happen to us, but life is what we make it. If we always play the victim, we go nowhere. By looking for the silver lining, we proactively choose to be positive and to learn and grow from the disappointment. I believe everything happens for a reason, which is why it doesn't pay to stress over things. There's always something to be gained from even the worst scenarios. We learn, we grow and we move on!

If you think today's a beautiful day because the sun is shining, would it be any less beautiful if the clouds rolled in? If your life is beautiful because everything is going well, would it be any less beautiful if some clouds rolled in? Like the weather, everything in our lives is subject to change. But also like the weather, when things look stormy, you can be assured that the sun will come out again eventually.

If you are a chronic worrier, consider foggy weather. Planes may take off in thick fog, but in time the pilots fly thousands of feet up to clear and beautiful skies, leaving the fog behind. Life is like that. At one level, we are groping in the fog. By simply rising above it, we have clarity. Next time you find yourself bogged with anxiety and worry, say to yourself, "I will think this thing through and not be disturbed by it." Practice this and you will find your worry has lost its power.

It's never easy navigating through difficult times in your life, but by learning what you can from adversity during those rainy times, you're helping build your character. We all would love each day to be sunny and carefree, but that's not the way life works. It's difficult to avoid becoming sour when life delivers more stress than you think you can handle. Just accept that you're going through a rough patch, and don't lose sight of your long-term goals. Don't fall into the "why me?" trap, but instead try to take proactive steps to ease yourself out of your predicament.

SUE SAYS

The happiest of people don't necessarily have the best of everything; they just make the most of everything that comes their way!

Learn to love what you see in the mirror

In our society, high value is placed on outward beauty. From advertising to beauty pageants to plastic surgeons promising to make us more beautiful, we learn from a young age that if we are attractive, we are a winner. Don't you think that we as a society should look beyond a pretty face? How about looking deeper to find who that person really is? We really need to acknowledge the beautiful inner qualities of people and teach our children from an early age that being beautiful on the inside is what really counts. Qualities such as respect, integrity and appreciation of others are, to me, what make a person beautiful. We all can make ourselves attractive from the outside. Makeup and other temporary fixes will definitely do that. But to be a person of quality will last our entire lifetime . . . long after our outward beauty fades.

It's a fact that your body confidence is based mostly on what you see when you look in a mirror. If you're like most people, the first thing you see is probably your least favorite body part. If this is true, don't worry—you're not alone! Here's why:

Advertisers spend an inordinate amount of money selling us on the concept of ideal beauty. Basically, we're being brainwashed. One of the most harmful activities is comparing your body to "better" bodies. The best way to do this is to read glossy magazines filled with photos of airbrushed models. We look at these images and know that these people are successful because of their bodies—and think that if we only looked like them, we'd be successful, too. We're all too painfully aware that we will never look like that. Our body confidence plummets, and thus, the spiral effect of hating what we see in the mirror! From your earliest days, whether you played with Superman or Barbie, you were receiving constant images of what beauty is supposed to look like.

If you don't like your features or your shape, your body confidence suffers, and you will feel inadequate in most areas of your life. If you can learn to love what you see in the mirror, your confidence will skyrocket, and you will put yourself in the spotlight where you belong. A great way to change every negative thought you have about your body is to take a look at each part and think about what it does for you. Adore your arms for their ability to hug a loved one; worship your legs for their ability to take you anywhere you want to go; love your eyes for their ability to see all the beauty that surrounds you; appreciate your lips because when they smile, your whole face lights up. Realize that your body is perfect in every way that truly matters.

We're all naturally attracted to visual beauty. Eye-catching ads with perfect models appeal to us—otherwise advertisers wouldn't spend so much money making them. In our everyday lives, however, it is important to keep in mind that outer beauty does not represent what is on the inside. We often dismiss those without a visual canvas of beauty and prefer those we believe have real beauty. I have met so many attractive people who are ugly on the inside and so many people who are beautiful on the inside but not so perfect on the outside. Don't be quick to dismiss someone who may not possess the perfect appearance. Perfection comes from within!

To improve your body confidence, there are two things you can do: You can change how you look, which is basically fruitless, or you can change how you *feel* about how you look. Sure, you can lose weight or build muscle on your frame (which is great because you'll be healthier, more energetic and in control), but it won't necessarily make you look like a movie star, which you may feel is necessary for you to really feel good about yourself. You must learn to love what you see no matter what "flaws" appear.

Visualize your body as your employee and you as the boss. It works hard every day for you and supports everything you do, from waking up to brushing your teeth. It's such a hard worker that it goes for 24 hours a day, seven days a week without stopping. That's one great employee! Now, are you a good boss? Do you treat this employee with respect? If you don't have body confidence, you probably treat this employee pretty badly, ignoring its hard work and just harping on its flaws. Try thanking it once in a while . . . by getting a nice massage, buying a new outfit or taking a walk in the park. Make a list of all the good things your body does: maybe you're a great dancer or a wonderful pianist. Add something to your list every day.

Here are some helpful tips to build your confidence with the body you were born with:

Look in the mirror, a really good look.

Think about all the compliments you've ever received. Maybe people tell you how great your hair is or how beautiful your eyes are. Maybe you have a nice smile. Try to see what other people see.

Find at least three things you like about yourself, and then accentuate them as you dress to go out. If you love your eyes, make sure your hair doesn't cover them up. If your hair is one of your assets, make sure it looks clean and vibrant. In short, magnify what you like. We can't change our gene pool. Maybe your genes make you short instead of tall, or you have a tendency to gain weight more easily than another person. This can't be changed, but you can learn to love yourself and make the most of what you can change, which is the attitude you show the world. Accept yourself for who you are, how you look, and focus on what really matters: the things about you that are unseen—your heart, your mind and your soul!

If you tend to be heavy due to an imbalance of eating and exercising, don't just give up, thinking that you can't change so you might as well keep eating the wrong things. You may think it doesn't impact your psyche, but not taking care of yourself will only make you feel worse about yourself. Try your best to make small, gradual improvements in your health. Even if you'll never be skinny, you can still treat the body you have with respect. Eventually you will love yourself more, because you will gain the self-respect that comes with having discipline and doing the right thing for you.

Remember, your body is a hard worker. Make sure you acknowledge it with your appreciation by giving it a raise!

Live in the present moment

The secret of health for both mind and body is not to mourn for the past, not to worry about the future, nor to anticipate troubles, but to live the present moment wisely and earnestly.

—Buddha

When I was a teenager and obsessed about what I perceived as dire emergencies, I remember an older friend of my parents saying, "Life goes very fast. Enjoy your teenage years, because before you turn around, you'll be my age!" I listened half-heartedly, my attention focusing on my current problem. Now that I am where that woman was, I realize she was right! Time flies. A friend and I were recently talking about how fast the year had gone by—how we couldn't believe another Thanksgiving and holiday season were already upon us! It made me pause to consider how much quality time we truly spend amid the clutter of errands and blur of activities we do blindly on a daily basis. Think about it: Our time here on Earth is very limited. Each day that isn't fully enjoyed is lost forever. Many people are so concerned with adding days to their life that they forget about adding life to their days! We won't live forever, and unless we stop wasting each day on petty nonsense, such as competing with others, holding on to resentment and staying stuck in a negative mindset, we will reach the end of our days and wonder where the time went. Focus on what really matters, and live as if each day is your last.

A lot of our stress comes from feeling that we are focusing and succeeding in one area of our life at the expense of other, more important areas. Success in one role doesn't justify failure in another. Being successful in your business can't justify failure in a relationship; success in social activities can't justify failure as a parent. The pieces of the pie have to be fairly equal or your life will never be in balance.

How many of us, when we are at the office, think about what we're going to do on the weekend? How many of us on the weekend think about what we have in store for us at work when we return? Moments come and go as we do our important tasks of the day. We're always thinking about what needs to be done. Quality moments slip by into the shadows of our life. They become lost and forgotten.

Practice being in the moment. Immerse yourself in whatever you are doing, whether it's washing the dishes or eating an apple. Experience the sensation of the water running on your hands, notice the sound of the apple crunching and the sweetness of the fruit. Completely let go. As you practice releasing the anxious thoughts that fill your head by being totally and completely in the moment, your anxiety and depression will cease to exist.

When you live in the moment, you notice and experience every event that occurs. Difficult to do? You bet. I often find my mind wandering off in other directions. The key is starting with baby steps. Become aware of what you are doing, be it driving, exercising or drinking your morning cup of coffee.

Think about events in your life you remember vividly. Those are times you were living in the moment! Even though many years may have passed, you still have a keen memory; you might remember every detail. These times could include a wedding day, a first love, the birth of a child. But living in the moment during special occasions is easy. Most days are not special occasions, and unless you learn to live in the moment, distractions will rob you of your life. Even if there is a long line at the grocery, don't let it upset you. Use the opportunity to notice the people around you, or to learn some patience! Every moment in life has a purpose, even the negative ones. Don't think about that doctor appointment you have next week. Focus on the scent of the air first thing in the morning or how beautiful the color of the flowers or the changing leaves are!

How can you start living in the moment? Some ideas:

Take a different route to your destination. Try a new road with a new view to get to the same place. Going a different way is an opportunity to concentrate on your surroundings.

Play a sport. When that ball is coming at you, there's no time to think about what bill you forgot to pay.

Pray or meditate. Both deliver a sense of peace, relax body and mind and can make you more intensely aware of self and surroundings.

Take a warm bubble bath. Play some soft music, relax and feel the warmth of the water. Now, that is enjoying the moment!

Take time to appreciate each day. Most people wait all week for Friday to arrive. Did they really enjoy the rest of the week, or were they eagerly trying to get through it in order to enjoy the weekend? The present moment is all we have. Stop from time to time and check in with what's going on around you right now. Tomorrow may not come, so enjoy every single day of the week to the fullest.

Keep a journal and at the end of the day, write about the moments when you were totally present. Review your journal weekly. This will encourage you to concentrate on what you're doing. Eventually, living in the moment will become a habit.

Don't delay the good stuff. Stop saving the good china for that special occasion. Stop saving that expensive outfit for an invitation that may never come. Every day you are alive is a special occasion. Every minute, every breath, is a gift!

Do something creative. Whether you paint, do woodworking, garden or play an instrument, you'll have to pay attention to your creation.

Do repetitive exercise. When the muscles are taxed, the mind follows. Focus on each movement, and you'll force your mind to live in that single moment with your body.

Have a sense of humor! People who are always preoccupied with worry or resentment usually don't smile much. Finding humor in life requires living in the moment in order to notice all the silly things that happen to us.

Don't wait for a milestone to be happy. If you'll be happy "when I buy my house" or "when I make more money," you aren't enjoying now. *Today* is the time of your life, a bright new day complete with 24 hours of opportunities and choices. This unique gift, this day, cannot be exchanged, replaced or refunded. Use it in good health and make the most of it! Don't hide away from the world. Try new things, meet new people. You only ever have *this* moment to live.

Accept what you can't change according to your schedule
If you find yourself spinning your wheels, trying to make something happen and repeatedly hitting a brick wall, stop for a moment. Relax.

When things look bleak and dark, work hard to find the light. No matter how bad it seems, staying stuck in self-pity and resentment will only drag you deeper into the darkness. It IS a choice. Life is filled with ups and downs, and resisting the downs will only exhaust you. Remember, life is fluid. The ups and downs are a given. Have the attitude that every bad situation is only temporary and trust that the tides will change—they always do!

Sometimes the best thing you can do is to stop trying so hard, stop trying to manipulate things to go your way. Let yourself just be. Accept things as they are. Find that gentle flow of life and go with it, not against the current. This doesn't mean that you stop taking responsibility for your life. Rather, it's about gently guiding your life in the direction you want instead of trying to force it to happen immediately.

Many times, things will come together or situations will improve when they are meant to as long as we are patient and accept the delays for what they are: temporary setbacks.

Work on overcoming your perfectionism

I admit it: I am a work in progress in terms of my perfectionism. I wouldn't say I'm a true perfectionist, but the tendency is there. I was told from very early on in my life that I was too hard on myself, and that no one is judging me except myself. I can't remember when I started thinking I had to be perfect, but I don't necessarily need to know where this belief came from in order to change it. Neither do you.

In its pathological form, perfectionism is a belief that any output less than perfect is unacceptable. A perfectionist doesn't enjoy the process, just the end result.

Black-and-white thinking is a hallmark of the perfectionist personality. They see most experiences as either good or bad, perfect or imperfect—nothing in between. There is a cost to this behavior: a high rate of depression among perfectionists, because their drive to be perfect always ends in disappointment. They tend to have negative attitudes and think if something can't be done perfectly, it's not worth doing.

The irony is, being a perfectionist will keep you from having a perfect life. When you believe you have to be 100 percent perfect, your nervousness and lack of confidence actually *make* you perform terribly. All you are focused on is what can go wrong.

For many years, people told me to start a blog and write down all the things I was knowledgeable about. But I hesitated because I thought, "Who would read it? I'm not a very good writer!" When we are so hard on ourselves, we often end up not doing anything at all for fear we will fail or be rejected. It's a Catch-22. You won't know that it's all going to work until you try, but fear of not being perfect keeps you from trying.

On the other side of the coin, fear of success is also scary for a perfectionist: "If I am successful, then I will have to maintain that success." This can be a real burden.

Now, there's a difference between being a perfectionist and a high achiever. A high achiever puts every effort into being the best he or she can be, but isn't obsessed with it. High achievers accept that making mistakes and possibly failing are part of the process.

If you struggle with perfectionism, here are some things to think about and to try:

Don't fall into the trap of limited happiness, telling yourself you'll be happy only when things are just right, or you are just right, or when you reach your goal (weight loss, a significant other, a child, a great promotion, retirement). If you pin your happiness on those situations, chances are you'll never be truly at peace. Remind yourself that making gradual progress in any endeavor is a reason to be happy and proud.

It's so difficult for many of us to feel content when things are not perfect. But if you really think about it, things will never be entirely perfect. So we must learn to look at what's good, not focus on what's not so good!

If you have someone in your present or past who makes you feel you have to prove yourself, or if you feel that your self-worth depends on that person, let that go. Realize that this person doesn't define who you are. Continue to set goals for yourself, but take it slow and don't give yourself a deadline.

Don't beat yourself up over something that could have been done better. Delete all the negative thoughts that run through your mind. You did the best you could. Treat yourself with respect. Forget about the mistakes you made in the past and move on. Nothing can change the past. Learn to laugh at yourself.

Stop calling yourself a failure. Take that word out of your vocabulary! Instead, look for the lesson during those times when you feel less than perfect. How about, "This is an opportunity to grow and improve in the future?" Remember, it takes courage to be resilient and try again and again.

Give yourself permission to be less than perfect. After all, if we were perfect, there'd be no place to go but down! Practice, yes, but if you never achieve perfection, at least enjoy the ride. Life's too short. Dare to be imperfect and, I promise, your life will be better for it!

Get professional help

When we think about addictions, we commonly picture a person who abuses alcohol, is dependent on drugs or gambles money away. We are not as likely to think about people who exercise too much, overindulge or underindulge in food, or can't stop shopping. Yet these things can create unhealthy balances and end up being as powerful and damaging as an addiction to a harmful substance.

If you are facing an addiction—if you feel out of control with a specific behavior and simply cannot stop—talk to someone. Ask for help. Many other people have experienced what you are going through, and help is available. You just have to ask. You are valuable and worthy, no matter how you may feel about yourself right now, so please don't give up on yourself. You matter!

Feelings of persistent sadness can sometimes take over our lives. We might just need a good cry to cleanse ourselves of the pain and sorrow and then feel rejuvenated. Often our beliefs create thoughts that contribute to our sadness. Work to eliminate these limiting beliefs from your life. Each new day is another opportunity to improve your life. No matter what is going on or who has hurt you, don't allow the sadness to define you and interfere with achieving your goals. Turn that frown upside down. We all need to see your beautiful smile! But we also need to understand that sometimes we can't identify and eliminate on our own the beliefs that make us sad. If sadness becomes a part of your life with no relief, professional help is needed. Seek it without hesitation. No matter how sad and hopeless you feel, depression can be helped. You're worth it!

Finding peace

We all want peace, but many of us believe that peace will come from foundations or organizations larger than we are. The opposite is true. Peace starts with each individual. It is crucial that we each create peace in the small and large moments of our lives, and live it in our words and actions.

3

Conditioning Yourself for Success

You can condition your mind to be successful, just as you can condition your body to be strong. You'll be amazed at the difference a change in thinking and attitude can make in your life once you do so. The principles I talk about in this chapter can apply to just about every situation life hands you.

Gratitude

Being grateful is a huge step toward happiness and joy. And there is always, always, always something to be thankful for!

Grateful people have more satisfaction in life, more energy and lower levels of depression and stress. Studies show that people who take a few minutes each day to write down the things they are grateful for sleep better, take better care of their bodies and generally have higher self-esteem.

When you're grateful for everything in your life—who you are, who you know and what you have—you feel uplifted. Even if things aren't going well, by focusing on what you are grateful for, you will bounce back more quickly from any negative situation.

How to cultivate a spirit of gratitude

Becoming grateful is about being aware of your surroundings and not taking anything for granted. By doing so, you'll find there are numerous times every day when you can exercise your thankfulness.

Just because we are alive, it doesn't mean everything is handed to us! If someone does something kind for you, try to reciprocate. Say thank you. This small gesture keeps you aware of what others do and how meaningful it is to you.

When you take time to show and tell others that you appreciate them, you not only get joy, you give joy, too. There are many things to appreciate others for: your mate, for giving you love; your children, for bringing laughter into your life; your boss, for hiring you and helping you earn a good income; even the person who holds the elevator for you! Take notice of these situations and your day will be great!

Consistently look for things and people to appreciate. A great ritual for getting your day started in the right way is to finish this statement: "Today, I am grateful for _____."

How many of us know people who seemingly have it all, but yet are still unhappy. These people make us realize that true happiness comes from within. How we feel about ourselves comes from deep within our core. It's not conditional, based on money, status, or material possessions. You don't need to wait for some great event to take place in order to find happiness. It doesn't have to be something specific. It all begins with taking control of your thoughts, which, in turn changes your outlook on life. There are little moments of happiness every single day. It's not all about a happy life . . . it's about the many happy moments that make up a life.

Sit down and make a list of all the things and people that you are grateful for. Carry it around with you for a while, and whenever you feel a bad mood coming on, take out your list and read it. See how it makes you feel. What's so great about writing down why you are grateful is that it doesn't take too much effort and can be very powerful. When you look back over what you are grateful for, you can see just how much you have and what you have accomplished. It is an amazing way to build your sense of worth.

Staying grateful when times are tough
If everything's going well, it's easy for us to feel positive and happy. But what about the tough times, the times that challenge us in seemingly every way? I believe there is always something about your situation for which you can be grateful. Even in difficult times, I try to find at least one thing to be thankful for. It's a great way to keep my attitude in check and get a little perspective.

Start with small things. Is there someone or something that touched your life today in a positive way, such as a stranger who smiled? Did some-one let you move into their lane in traffic? Are you healthy? Loved?

Is there a silver lining in the very thing that is challenging you? Your job may not be the best, but at least you have a job. Someone may have hurt you; think about all the other people in your life who have not. Be grateful that times change, and things resolve eventually—probably sooner than you think they will. It's so hard to have perspective when you're in the thick of it. Being thankful can unlock powerful feelings of happiness and peace that will energize you, even when things are not perfect.

I recently had the unfortunate experience of having a scratched cornea. The pain was unbearable, and every single aspect of my day was a blur except for the intense pain in my eye. We tend to be grateful each day for things like a successful business venture, maybe a fun lunch date, and great weather. But how many of us are grateful for the fact that we can go through the day pain-free?

A poor person who lives in the moment and enjoys life is more blessed than a sick and worried millionaire. So enjoy every minute of this short life, because it comes your way only once. Be grateful for being alive in a state of sound mind, body and spirit. And remember that no matter what you are going through, someone else out there is going through something worse. Reflect on little blessings in your life and be thankful!

Some days everything just seems to go wrong, or so it seems. We feel like there's a black cloud over us and nothing will ever go right. When this happens, take a deep breath and put things in perspective. If you need some help with gaining perspective, just listen to the morning news. It's filled with tragedy after tragedy. Life is definitely not perfect, and sometimes it can really take its toll. But, we must always remember that we are alive and life is a gift. No matter how difficult your situation, it could always be worse. Don't wait until a tragedy to appreciate what you have NOW. Don't worry so much about the future. Look at all you have today and be grateful.

Change an attitude of ingratitude by imagining, just for a minute, how empty your life would be without your blessings. So often, we fail to appreciate our loved ones and all of the gifts of the universe until it is too late and they are gone. An expression of gratitude toward grandparents, children, spouses, co-workers, and even the bus driver, can release you from the boredom trap. Stop taking life for granted and live with appreciation.

Don't delay your thankfulness

I used to be superstitious, thinking that if I felt thankful that everything was going well, this would automatically jinx the situation. I would suppress my feelings of gratitude and hide them somewhere deep inside. Of course, this was a foolish belief, and I was only starving myself of the wonderful feelings that ensue from being outwardly grateful and happy. Having gratitude does not bring bad luck. It actually opens the door for good luck to flow in! Now I am quick to say thank you for all the good that comes to me, even the very small ones. Make it a point every day to say "Thank you for all the blessings in my life." It is very difficult to be miserable and grateful at the same time.

It's great to have goals and to visualize and work toward reaching them. For your own happiness, be sure to take time along the way to appreciate things you have now and what you have already accomplished. We often think that once we reach our goal—whether it's getting that promotion, nabbing that special client or even winning the lottery—then we will be content. But what about the phone call from your friend/spouse/child telling you he or she is thinking of you? What about the fact that your parents are still alive and healthy? What about the sun coming out after a few days of rain? We often take all this for granted in our blind rush to achieve success. When you are grateful, you appreciate everything in your life. Nothing is taken for granted.

A great quote attributed to Dr. Seuss says, "Don't cry because it's over, smile because it happened." We all have regrets about things from our past that we wish we could have done or reacted to differently . . . or wish we had never done at all! Every day we learn and grow, and what we thought was wonderful yesterday may not seem so great today. That doesn't mean that we should regret our choice, for that is how we learn, grow and evolve into our authentic self. So, today, delete the "should have's" and "might have's," and don't regret a single thing. Smile and be thankful because it happened.

Savor each beautiful moment. Many of us are too rushed to enjoy life, too confused to be simple, too rich to ever have enough, too worried to be healthy, too ungrateful to be happy, and too controlling to be free. There are simple things in life that bring joy. Do your part today to respect what is in front of your nose . . . a beautiful day filled with simple pleasures.

Pay it forward! There are very few feelings that surpass that of knowing you've helped someone—whether it's through a financial donation, a mentoring program, or giving up your seat on a crowded bus. It feels good, and in fact, it's good for you! Research has found that the effect of giving—it doesn't matter how little or how much—is similar to the so-called runner's high. Both produce a pleasurable gush of endorphins (brain chemicals). But unlike exercise euphoria, this feeling lasts longer. Here's the evidence: 90 percent of people who regularly give to others rate their health a better grade than those who don't. Helping others helps you. It strengthens your immune system, boosts positive emotions, decreases pain, and provides stress relief. Separate studies show that heart attack patients who are charitable recover faster than those who aren't, and those who do volunteer work have death rates 60 percent lower than those who don't. It's a win-win situation!

Celebrate all that is going well!

It's not always the grandiose events or big things that should excite us. Let's get excited about life in general! Applaud your own brilliance, your unique style, your family, your clean closets! Celebrate anything and everything that lifts you up. If you find one thing to celebrate every day, your mind will soon automatically look for things to celebrate. It's like you have a searchlight within you that zeros in on only the good.

Happiness is not an end result. It is about enjoying the process. Thinking that happiness is something we have to chase or achieve blurs us to what is happening now. It's about being able to enjoy the not-so-perfect times along the way, and realizing that life is unfolding as it should. If things are not going as well as you would hope, keep your chin up. Have faith that tomorrow will be a better day and enjoy what you have today!

Celebrate frequently! Valentine's Day only comes once a year, so don't wait for that one special day to show your appreciation and gratitude for the one you love. Do it every day. It's so easy to forget to say "thank you" and "I love you." Learn to shower your partner with gratitude so he or she always feels loved and appreciated. Your partner will love you for it. And your love will flourish.

Sadness, anger, and frustration come when we aren't grateful for the simple things in life—a smile, a touch, a hug, the smell of turkey cooking, the smell of the ocean, the favorite songs we listen to when we're down. When we actively reflect on how grateful we are for these things in our lives, we reconnect to our authentic selves. By being grateful, the negatives don't seem so bad, for we see that there's usually a larger purpose behind them, a purpose that will help us grow and develop.

Holidays are a great time to remember everything that's good in your life. On my birthday, instead of adding up the years, I try to think about special people who love me and care, and others who've enriched my life just by being there. Passing years will never mar the memories of experiences that have made you who you are. Next time you cut your cake, instead of counting candles, count your blessings!

SUE SAYS

Set your personal GPS (Gratitude Positioning System). Follow the arrows to your mirror and stop to tell yourself how wonderful and talented you are. All day, notice the landscape of your life and be grateful for the smallest thing. Gratitude isn't the result of happiness, it's the cause of happiness. You have reached your destination!

Confidence

Working with my wonderful life coaching clients has given me a lot of insight into the process of success. Regardless of our background, skills or experience, we can't be successful until we feel confident about who we are and what we're doing. We mistakenly think that if we're successful, we will then be confident. It's just the opposite! Feeling confident first opens the door to success and achieving our goals. Others take their cue from you. If you are confident, people will have confidence in you. If you seem hesitant and unsure, no one will feel comfortable putting trust in you. We all have strengths. Make a list, even the smallest things, of what you do well. Even if it's making a great cup of coffee or being able to cross your eyes, notice how you feel about it. That feeling is confidence. Just like rabbits, the feeling of confidence multiplies fast when you start paying attention to your strengths instead of your weaknesses.

It's no secret that confidence is key to success in life. Confidence, not status, is ultimately attractive to others. If you were looking to start a relationship, would you be attracted to someone who seemed timid and always looking for positive affirmation? When you're confident, you believe you're capable of doing anything—which perpetuates more confidence, impressing others and bringing you success.

Confidence isn't arrogance or gloating. It's not about purposely drawing attention to yourself. Rather, confident people project confidence by directing their focus and attention outward. They feel no need to assert themselves or their qualities unnecessarily.

Genuinely confident people are usually calm and self-assured, and don't need to toot their horns. They are aware of their own worth, whether or not the spotlight is on them.

Self-confidence is a choice. On those days when you feel insecure or powerless, remind yourself that you're in charge. You can choose how you feel.

Basically, confidence isn't about changing who you are, but about changing how you see yourself and how you present yourself to others. And it can be practiced.

How to make a good first impression

When you meet someone for the first time, it takes only a moment for them to form an opinion about you. Their opinion is based in part on what you're wearing, but also on your body language, your demeanor, your mannerisms, your voice and even your posture. The way you handle those first encounters is extremely important.

If you were standing in an echo chamber and said the words, "I am a failure" or "I will never be happy," how would it feel to hear your words bouncing right back at you? Every thought and action we produce is much like an echo. What you send out comes right back to you! Pay attention to how you talk to yourself and to others. If you project positive thoughts, you will get them back. Your positive echo will reverberate on and on. Today, make it a point to yell out "I am capable of anything I put my mind to." The energy that will bounce back to you will make it possible. Always listen to your own echo. If you don't like what you're hearing, then change it.

Try to be open and confident. Use your body language to project self-assurance. Stand tall, smile, make eye contact, greet with a firm handshake. All of this will help you project confidence. If you're calm and confident, the other person will feel more at ease, too.

If this is difficult for you, practice some positive visualization. See yourself walking into meetings feeling confident and self-assured, see how positively others react to you and remember how that feels. Imagine taking control and people respecting you and your opinion. Feel the self-empowerment that comes with this scenario.

Always make eye contact when speaking to another person. Someone who stares at the floor when spoken to projects the image of being meek. Also, when shaking hands, make sure your grip is strong; a limp handshake delivers the wrong message. I know of employers that, when interviewing potential employees, look for these traits as signs of whether or not they should be hired. So keep this in mind: It's all a game. Even if you don't really believe it, you can fake an image of confidence. The more you fake it, the more you will eventually start believing that you do have confidence.

You represent your personal brand. According to an important study by Albert Mehrabian, a well-known professor of psychology at UCLA, appearance is 55 percent of a first impression. If your appearance gives the wrong impression, you are already at a disadvantage. Another 38 percent is based on your voice. If your voice is weak or harsh, your chances of making a good first impression are diminished. Your actual message is responsible for a mere 7 percent of your first impression. Get the first 93 percent wrong and no one is listening!

Pretend your way into confidence

Sometimes, a person's confidence is nothing but a façade. Often we see someone walk in with a self-assured smile and determined posture, and can't see that deep down, he or she is shaking at the knees. For instance, I was once chosen to go onstage to assist a performer. My initial reaction was complete and total *terror*. I don't know what propelled me onto the stage, but somehow I got there. I was onstage for at least 30 minutes, and at the end of the show, everyone came up to me and told me I was a natural. They couldn't see the fear and insecurity that was inside me because I projected a different demeanor on the outside.

The best way to project confidence is to ACT as if you're brimming with confidence—even if you're not. This is the strategy used by most people you meet, who are really insecure but act as if they are secure.

I read an article about Meryl Streep that really surprised me. She said when she is about to embark on a new movie shoot, she often has strong feelings of inadequacy and self-doubt. Thoughts swirl around her head such as, "I'm not a good actress" and "What am I doing? I'll never be able to pull this off." This from Meryl Streep, who is considered by many to be one of the greatest film actresses, who has played the lead in some of the best movies ever made! She went on to share her strategy for overcoming self-doubt: "Fake it till you make it." Feel the fear and do it anyway. She says she shows up and gives it her all. She doesn't let her self-doubt and inner critic paralyze her. She walks toward and through the fear and does her best work.

When I tell people that I have experienced many of the same insecurities and ups and downs that they feel, they're shocked. I have learned to heal, learned to project confidence, and learned, most of all that you can't judge a book by its cover. I've also learned that you're not alone. No matter how bad or embarrassed you feel about your own situation, there will be others out there experiencing the same emotions. When you hear yourself say "I am alone," it's your limiting inner voice trying to sell you a lie so you will remain stagnant. You and only you can solve your problems and make the changes necessary to improve your life. I can be a guide, and if you need my help, I am here. But ultimately, you must take control. If I can do it, so can you!

Most people aren't as secure as you think. There are many threats to self-confidence. We each want to be the ideal person, so we struggle to be wealthy, healthy, smart, funny and have a strong character. If we fall short in any of these areas, it wears away at our confidence. Don't worry. There is nothing wrong with you if you feel this way. We all have the same thoughts.

Do you get nervous when meeting new people in social situations? Be gentle with yourself. If you look around, those who are engaged in conversation, with others being drawn to them, seem like they really have it together. But confident people are not always people who have achieved perfection. Rather, confident people know they have flaws and shortcomings, but they have decided to like themselves anyway. They don't see limitations and failures as something built into their character.

In his autobiography, *Stories I Only Tell My Friends,* actor Rob Lowe talks about growing up in Malibu with his single mom and two brothers with very little money and very few luxuries. His friends, however, were privileged. One day, he was invited to a party thrown by one of the girls he knew. His mom didn't have the money to buy him a fancy suit, or even a decent belt. He ended up wearing a camera strap as a belt! Fortunately for him, he was very self-confident and walked into the party with the swagger of James Bond. He had a crowd of girls asking where he got the cool belt. When it comes to confidence, reality isn't important. Fake confidence can override the real turmoil going on inside you. People will pick up positive signals from your confident body language, expressions, eye contact, posture, and so on. It doesn't matter if you are wearing a paper bag—if you project self-confidence, you will be the star in any room you enter.

The amazing thing is that tasting the experience of confidence can lead a person to become confident for real! Pretending to be self-assured, even for a moment, shows you how easy it is and how great the rewards are. So the next time that you are feeling some social anxiety, remember: Fake it till you make it!

Start encouraging yourself with positive self-talk. Rephrase what you say to yourself. Instead of saying, "I struggle with self-confidence," switch your brain and language to say, "Until now, I haven't felt too confident, but from now on, I feel very self-assured and competent to handle anything that comes my way." Train your brain to picture a successful outcome and watch it happen. Your brain believes what you tell it.

Discouragement affects all of us from time to time. We all get the feeling that no matter what we do, it's a waste of effort. Accept that feeling for exactly what it is—a temporary state. Know that you will soon overcome this feeling and return to a more positive state. Even when others discourage you, even if events turn negative, know that your value is still there. You are talented and special. Our value is in who we are deep down, and if we continually praise ourselves for our unique qualities, our discouragement will have less space in which to grow.

When my son was little, he was very attached to his security blanket. Over time, the blanket became really frayed and raggedy, but he wouldn't go anywhere without it. In fact, I couldn't get him to sleep without it. We went on a vacation and on the way to the airport I realized that I forgot to take the blanket! I panicked, because I knew that this was going to be the end of our plan for a relaxing time. As soon as we got on the plane, he asked for his blankie. I told him that blankie was at home watching his toys, and then awaited a dreaded screaming tantrum. Well, guess what? He was fine! He looked out the window and was mesmerized by the flight. I realized that he has been ready to give up his security blanket all along! He now felt secure in himself, ready to move on without the aid of a ragged piece of cloth. Many of us are still holding on to our security blankets, afraid to move out of our comfort zones. What's holding you in situations and actions that no longer work for you? Until you can let go of those old, outdated habits, they'll continue to hold you prisoner. To stay in your comfort zone through habit, or an irrational fear of what may lie outside, will only keep you trapped in a life of frustration and regret. One single action will allow you to open the door of your self-imposed prison and walk out a free person. Let go of your security blanket and see the opportunities that await you.

Choose your friends wisely

Some people need an entourage of "friends" around them on a constant basis. They believe that by projecting an image of popularity, others will respect them more. What's so sad is that, in reality, these people are so busy with the image that they never cultivate a real and lasting friendship. In the end, it's quality, not quantity, that we should consider when choosing who we befriend. I have learned that real friends are priceless. They uplift, accept and correct when necessary. They understand and accept our shortcomings and forgive when we disappoint. Above all, they love us and show it!

The people we associate with have a great impact on our lives. Are you allowing the very best people into your life? Believe it or not, the types of people we hang with affect us in many ways, and depending on who they are, the effect can be positive or negative. Think about it. If you hang around with people who have no class or values, eventually that is going to rub off on you. However, if you hang around people who value intelligence, good manners and integrity, that will rub off on you, too. Which would you choose? Stay with those that inspire you to reach higher, not those who may, inadvertently, drag you down to their level.

Have you ever noticed that some people just rub you the wrong way for no apparent reason? And that you're drawn to others and don't know why? I believe that people we respond to strongly are only mirrors of ourselves. You cannot love or hate something about another person unless it reflects something you love or hate about yourself. The next time you have a strong feeling about another person, take into consideration what traits they own that mirror yours. It will surprise you. Looking at yourself through your perception of others can be an eye-opening experience. Be loving and respectful to all people, and you will attract individuals who will love and respect you back. By showcasing our best always, we are allowing the goodness we see in others be our mirror.

Be aware of who you are spending time with, because the habits of others can be contagious. For instance, if you're the smartest person in your group of friends, then you need to enlarge your group. If the people you surround yourself with tend to be negative and destructive, you need to move on. Changes in life can be difficult, but they're necessary if you are to move forward and grow. Sometimes, this means that you need to change the people who are around you the most. Develop new friendships with people who will help you rise by inspiring you with their own greatness.

Surround yourself with people with whom you share a mutual respect. A good friendship can do wonders for your confidence if the other person enjoys what you have to say. When another person thinks you're cool, you'll begin to notice it, too.

If you stay around someone who doesn't appreciate your gifts and talents, you'll be in a constant battle that will eventually sap your energy and enthusiasm. You don't have to prove yourself to anyone. Your job is to be you. Steer clear of critics. Surround yourself with friends who champion your self-worth, cheer you on with vigor and make you feel good about yourself. (You, in turn, should do the same for them!)

We all have a purpose in life. You may think you don't, but please listen. Your purpose has nothing to do with your job, your social standing or your bank account. Maybe your purpose is to share your wit with others; maybe it's your positive disposition that makes people happy just to be around you. Never listen to the false belief that you are not important and that what you do is meaningless. You are one of the bricks that holds this universe together. We need you!

Sometimes I feel as if many of the people in my life and come and go, like a revolving door. They—and I—meet and move on. So be it! Everyone who comes into our life is there for a reason. Some cross our path for a very short time because they needed us for a life lesson. Others come into our life and stay as a lasting friendship. Still others enter our path at breakneck speed, disturbing our peace of mind and bringing negative and destructive energy. We then need to clear the path to regain our positive energy.. The true friends are the ones that know your faults and accept you for who you are. You bring out the best in each other. You can count on them and they can count on you. Don't hold on to people if you are just an option in their life. Everyone, even the negative influences, taught you a lesson. Don't be sad, but be grateful for every person that has been a part of your life. They may have been there for a season, but they were there for a reason!

Pay attention to the physical attributes that boost confidence
When you look good, you feel good. It just is a fact. You have a certain spring in your step and even talk differently. When this occurs, people respond to you differently. So change your eating habits and start exercising! This will do wonders for your confidence.

Always look your best—even if you work from home, are a stay-at-home mom or have no real impetus to care about your appearance. You'll respect yourself more and be ready for whatever the day brings, including answering the door when opportunity knocks.

Whether you realize it or not, your body language is a huge factor in how you are perceived. Stand up straight and lose the slouch. Standing erect with shoulders relaxed sends a message of self-confidence and pride.

Finally, smile! Not smiling makes you unapproachable. So stand tall, smile and make new friends!

Keep learning, always

Are you good at making small talk in social situations? One of the most important elements in honing your social skills is having the ability to make small talk and turn any conversation into an interesting one. Try to stay current about common topics like music, film, art, technology, world and national issues. And try some humor. It's a surefire way of breaking the ice in any social event.

Learn something new every day and share your opinion. When new, unfamiliar subjects come up in conversation, genuinely ask about them. Strike up conversations with people who cross your path, even the cashier at the grocery store or the bank teller. Sharpening your social skills this way is great practice for those times when you are in an unfamiliar situation, such as not knowing anyone at a party.

In the past, were you great at something—maybe a sport— and gave it up? Nothing stops you from going back and trying it again. It may give a real boost to your sense of well-being and, even if you're not as good as you were before, your confidence will soar just for trying it again! And you'll have fun!

SUE SAYS

The greatest gift is to learn to admit when you are wrong, move on because no one is perfect, and build bridges instead of walls.

Self-love and self-confidence

It's such an old saying, but it's true: You have to like yourself before you can expect anyone else to like you.

Write down a list of your strengths. Think of at least ten things you do well. I'm sure you can find them if you try. Focusing on your assets will make you feel better about yourself, which will result in your feeling more confident.

We all need to boost our confidence in one way or another. The trick is improving what you need to improve. Then life will become something you can handle with more ease. So go ahead—take the ball and start running!

Attitude

Always project a positive, winning attitude. Let go of the past, live in the moment and expect good things to happen. Try to stay around others who are positive, as that is contagious.

Either you control your attitude or it controls you. Yes, there are challenges, and life isn't always easy. But each day we wake up, we get another opportunity to make today better than yesterday. We get to uplift, inspire, encourage and impact others. We have this life. Let's make the most of it by remembering that life is a gift and not an obligation!

In 1966, the Beach Boys recorded the song "Good Vibrations." When we pick up good vibrations, we are attracting positive energy. It takes energy to laugh and smile. It's also contagious. When you smile at people, they will usually smile back. When you laugh, others follow. You are sending out good vibrations, and those around you—those who are open to good vibrations—pick them up.

Choose a positive outlook on life

We have a choice every day regarding the attitude we will embrace for that day. We can't always choose what happens to us. The only thing we can do is play on the one string we have, and that is our attitude. I'm convinced that life is 10 percent what happens to me and 90 percent how I react to it. And so it is with you. We are in charge of our attitudes.

Sometimes unpleasant things happen. Not everything works out. There are losses and failures, problems in relationships, more bills than money, challenging times at our workplaces. Again, we don't always have control over these events, but we can control our attitudes. When we see only closed doors, we're asking for frustration. But if we move our sight away from these things long enough, we might be surprised to discover a new row of open doors.

In fact, open doors are all around us. If you remain open-minded, positive and happy, then it's much easier to detach yourself from your problems and to see more clearly the new doors that open for you.

Do you ever wake up with a knot in your stomach for no apparent reason? This form of free-floating anxiety occurs when your brain thinks there is some apparent threat to your well-being. Try to identify if there truly is something that is worrying you. If you can't identify it, then realize that your anxiety is just an imagined fear. Retrain your brain to think positive. Even if things aren't perfect in your life, don't think of worst-case scenarios. The knot of anxiety doesn't help resolve your problems. In fact, it blocks your ability to think clearly. Keep focused on the fact that you are doing the best you possibly can, know you can deal with any challenge that comes your way, and that knot will unravel in no time!

With a positive outlook, you'll be able to find the good that may come out of a bad situation. For instance, if you lose your job, think of it as your opportunity to get a better one—maybe one you'll enjoy more.

Life is all about perception. We can all see the same movie, but each of us will see it differently through the lens of our unique experiences. We go through similar situations differently, based on what we think is true or valuable. Our lives can be full of joy or empty with despair. When we choose to be open to positive forces, we open ourselves to the magnificence of this life.

Cultivate your own contentment

Contentment is emphasizing what's good, not bad, and being thankful for what we have. It's being patient till we reach our goal. We can't always be ecstatic, but we can stay content by knowing we're doing the best we can even when things are not going well. This can become a lifestyle when you realize it takes time to achieve anything worthwhile, and that most problems are resolved in good time.

If we could just learn to be content—whatever that means personally for each of us—our stress levels would go down. Our health would improve. Our lives would feel richer.

If you have been giving your primary attention to your trials, and not to what's going well, it may not be easy to get out of that mode. You're used to thinking that way. Tell yourself, "Let it go." Let go of your problems for a little while and think about the opposite—everything that's good. Make the choice. Like anything else, the more you practice this, the easier it will get.

SUE SAYS

Happiness is not a gift delivered to our door each morning. Our circumstances are a small part of what makes us joyful. If we wait for them to be just right, we will never find lasting joy. It's from within. Our minds are banks, and if we regularly deposit encouraging, uplifting thoughts and bite our lips right before we begin to complain, we will find that we are truly rich!

Develop a childlike spirit

It's amazing how children can delight in building sandcastles, running around with their buckets filled with sand and making their mounds higher and higher. When a giant wave rides over their creation, they giggle and cheerfully start again to rebuild. There's no regret—just excitement for the next project, a new start, as they intuitively embrace ups and downs as natural parts of life.

When you get frustrated with your life, when a giant wave washes out the sandcastle you've been laboring over, be resilient. Laugh or shrug and start again. Try to look at your situation in a light-hearted way. No matter how much we worry about things, there are certain things over which we have no control. We can only choose to be happy now . . . and there will never be a time when it isn't now.

Expect good things to happen to you

When I go by myself to an event where I might know only one or two people, instead of worrying about whether anyone will like me or talk to me, I just assume that I will be liked.

Make expecting good things to happen to you a habit and it will change how you view the world. Unfamiliar situations become far less menacing. Most of the time, people are friendly to those who show interest and are open to communication.

There have been occasions in the past when, if I had to attend alone, I would worry about feeling out of place. I was so stressed out by the time I arrived that it took a glass of wine to relax me. Now, I just assume it will be easy and there will be someone fabulous to talk to. It always works!

It's all in the attitude. If you sit in a corner, you are sending a message that you are not confident. Walk around the room with your head held high and people will wonder if they can be lucky enough to meet you!

All you need to do to begin effortlessly attracting and experiencing your most desired dreams and visions for your life is to stop worrying about the outcome. Worrying only robs you of your strength. Instead, believe in the best possible outcome—and that is what you'll attract.

We were recently invited to an event that was quite a distance away from our home. It sounded quite interesting, so we decided to go. When we got there after a long drive, we realized that it was not what we expected and decided to just turn around and go home. As we were leaving, I got a call from someone telling me about another event nearby. We went, met wonderful people, and had a real blast! We should always realize that while these speed bumps may be disguised as life's interruptions and annoyances, there is always a reason for them. Nothing is an accident, it's a gift in disguise. Every moment of our day shifts, and we must believe in the blessings and significance of these shifts. The universe is showing us the way. We just have to recognize that!

Keeping a positive attitude when things go wrong

A person's true character is revealed in times of adversity. We all have been tested in one way or another. Each of us reacts differently to setbacks, but it is our behavior that determines if we continue on the road ahead or turn back in self-pity.

Always choose the appropriate attitude and action that will allow you to make the best out of a bad situation. The ability to do this plays an important role in your success.

Whether we realize it or not, every bad situation has at least one positive aspect. There usually is a silver lining somewhere, if you choose to see it! Even if you feel like your world is crumbling, look up to the sky and find the ray of hope.

A few years ago, I was driving back to New Jersey from Pennsylvania with my three boys, who were 12, 10 and 5 at the time. We had plans to meet my husband at a restaurant for dinner. The trip is no longer than 45 minutes, so we didn't bother to stock the car with the usual snacks. Cruising along I-95, things were going well until—dead stop! We assumed there was an accident and that we'd be moving shortly. Turns out there was a major oil spill from a tanker that jackknifed, and the police completely stopped traffic until they could clear it up. There was absolutely nowhere to go. We were stuck for hours!

The kids started screaming that they were hungry, rummaging through the car for anything they could find (unfortunately, that was some old jellybeans stuck in the pocket of the seat!). Finally, people on the highway started getting out of their cars. Folks started offering food and drink they had in coolers. Some shared cell phones with those who didn't have them and needed to make calls. And some even began playing musical instruments! There was a tailgate party feel in the air. This situation, which should have been a complete nuisance, turned into something enjoyable because of the choices we all decided to make: to meet new people, to laugh about the situation and to dance to the music! Eventually, the road opened up and we went our own ways. Amazingly, I am still in touch with some of the people I met that day on I-95 in Philadelphia!

When something goes wrong, don't let yourself get needlessly stressed, angry or upset. Stay calm. Take control of your emotions and move forward. Many times, situations we think are terrible are usually pretty insignificant when looking at the big picture. The worst thing that happened to me that day on the highway was that our dinner was delayed a few hours. How bad is that? A good sense of humor is also a necessity in seeing something humorous in the most annoying of circumstances.

Challenges and changes in your life are temporary detours. If you keep yourself headed in the right direction, and follow the detour, you still will reach your destination. It may not be easy, but in those times of struggle you will find a stronger sense of who you are. During those days of frustration and unexpected detours, remember to believe in yourself and all you want your life to be.

If you can't find the good, make the good!

A pearl is a beautiful thing produced as a result of an injury to the oyster. Sometimes, the treasure of our life in this world is also produced by an injury. If we'd never been wounded, if we hadn't been injured, then we could not produce our pearl.

Success doesn't come in one size only. Perhaps you lent an ear to a friend in need or finished a small task that was on your "to do" list. Maybe you made the decision to change a bad habit. Success is taking positive action . . . nothing more.

It's not easy to stay "unsour" in our lives, especially when we're handed circumstances that are most unfair. But if we keep squeezing those lemons we get into that pitcher called life and add a little sugar, our supply of happiness and joy will never run dry. If life has handed you lemons, how about starting your own lemonade stand? Hand out some lemonade to yourself as well as others. Positivity can quickly spread and make bad situations better for everyone..

Goals and Motivation

> *Today is your day! Your mountain is waiting. So get on your way.*
> —Dr. Seuss

In their ads, Nike coined the phrase, "Just do it." Life is short, and there is no better time than NOW to start toward your goal—big or small.

If you want something badly enough, make an attempt. If you want to advance your career, decide where you want to be and determine what steps will take you there. If you want to lose weight, study how you're currently eating and exercising and determine what needs to change and how. If you want to dance or sing, sign up for dance lessons or a singing coach. Take action. Persist, be determined, work at it. Just do it—whatever it is, whomever it involves—and put your all into it.

We were born to reach all the potential that is within us. It's not just in some of us; it's in all of us! And each one of us decides what he or she will do with that potential. As we let our own light shine, we automatically give others permission to do the same. Our actions can inspire others. You may even become someone else's role model!

Success starts when you begin to pursue it. You don't need to know all the answers in advance; you just need a clear idea of what your goal is. Don't procrastinate. Break problems into parts, and handle one part at a time. Divide your big plan into small steps and take that first step right away. Everyone who ever got where they are had to begin somewhere. Your big opportunity is where you are right now.

Getting started

In the Star Wars movie *The Empire Strikes Back*, the Jedi master Yoda says, "No! Try not. Do, or do not. There is no try." How often have we said "I'll try" when aiming at a goal? The fact is, either you will do it or you won't. There really is no trying, as Yoda pointed out. Either you will pick up that cookie or you won't. Either you will make that phone call or you won't. Either you will start an exercise routine or you won't. There is no in-between.

Decide that today is the day. Today, you will believe in your ability and take the first step. Today, you will remove the words "can't" and "impossible" from your vocabulary. Today, you will look at yourself in the mirror and say, "I can do it, and I will do it." Your six-minute mile is waiting for you, and it's up to you whether you break your personal record or merely walk in the slow lane and let others pass you by. Action makes it happen!

The Chinese philosopher Lao-tzu wrote, "A journey of a thousand miles begins with a single step." Setting an extreme goal is fine for the long term, but you're more likely to succeed—and to enjoy the journey—with a series of smaller, incremental goals. If you have any fear that you might not reach the goal you have planned, break it up into baby steps. Instead of trying to run a mile, start with a quarter-mile. Instead of trying to write a novel, write five pages in the next three days. Progress doesn't have to come in miles. Be realistic and build in a little comfort where you need it. If you don't enjoy it, you won't reach your goal!

Write down your goals and what steps you will take to achieve them. Go ahead and aim high. When you climb a tall ladder, you take one step at a time to eventually reach the top. Start each goal with "I WILL . . . ." Not "I hope to" or "I will try to." If you write "I will," you're more likely to follow through. Take one goal at a time, choose one step at a time and don't worry—life will take care of itself!

Instead of striving for perfection when reaching for your goal, strive for progress. Strive to better yourself by pushing yourself forward in a healthy and productive way. Something worth doing is worth doing poorly, at least at the beginning. Give yourself permission to fail and not to be perfect the first time. Learn from your actions and figure out how to do better the next time. It's so much more liberating and effective to learn from what happens than to beat yourself up over it.

Finally, set a deadline for your goal. Time is a one-way street—you can't make a U turn. Time is the most valuable commodity we have, so we must make the best use of it. Each hour that passes by is gone and will never return. Don't let time slip away when it comes to meeting your goal.

The mother of one of my clients decided to go back to school at age 45, to pursue a master's degree that would eventually lead to a new career. The program she entered required four years of full-time study. When people around her expressed concern that she would put her professional life on hold for so long, she told them, "In four years, I'll be 49 either with or without a new degree. I choose with." Time will pass one way or another, so why not use it to make the changes you want in your life?

Strive for your deadline, but don't be unnecessarily hard on yourself if you fail to meet it. Stay flexible. Goals are meant to be achieved; sometimes, along the way, the timeline may get delayed. It doesn't matter. Eventually it will happen.

Years ago, our family went to Acadia National Park for a vacation. We wanted to hike up Cadillac Mountain, but first we had to consider which level was appropriate for us. We chose an easier route, took our time and ended up at the top right alongside the folks who took the steeper path. Your journey to reaching your goals may take longer than you wish, but by knowing clearly what you want and planning every step carefully, you will get there. So find your mountain, select your path and start climbing.

Envision and expect success

You get what you expect. If I said to myself, "There's no way I will ever be a good Life Coach," my brain would look for reasons not to be one. You must believe in the best outcome. You family and friends may believe in you, but their opinion is worth nothing. Work on believing in yourself, and let go of needing others to believe in you. As soon as you start believing in yourself, others will see the star that you are!

Believe in your goal. We often say, "I'll believe it when I see it." Actually, when it comes to goals, the opposite applies: You need to believe it first and then you will see it. Look around. Everything you see didn't exist at one point in time. Someone had to envision it, believe they could produce it and then work to make it happen. They believed it first, and then worked at it until they succeeded.

Most of us have attention deficit disorder when it comes to achieving what we want. We give too much attention to creating our own misery by focusing on the detours, roadblocks, distractions, less important things, excuses. Energy flows where attention goes, so keep your attention focused on your intention! Jim Carrey wrote himself a check for $10 million, payable for services rendered, before he became famous. He envisioned success first. And if you put your attention on what you want to achieve, you'll do the same.

You can fine-tune your mental preparation further by incorporating affirmations and visualization into your efforts. Most great athletes, surgeons and artists use these tools consciously or subconsciously to enhance their skills. Nelson Mandela wrote in his autobiography how visualization helped him maintain a positive attitude while being imprisoned for 27 years: "I thought continually of the day when I would walk free. I fantasized about what I would like to do." He harnessed the power of his mind to sustain him. In the same way, you can harness yours to help you believe in yourself, stay focused on the outcome you want and remain persistent along the way.

Imagine your goals in the form of a movie trailer, an advance screening of the real you being brought to life. Visualizing your goals allows you to explore and discover what you could do if you let go of your limitations. Your mental trailer is full of possibility. You are more than capable of bringing out the best in yourself through your envisioned goals.

Don't limit yourself

Interesting fact: Koi, when put in a fish bowl, will only grow up to three inches. Placed in a large tank, they will grow to about nine inches long. In a pond, koi can reach lengths of eighteen inches and, amazingly, when placed in a lake, koi can grow to three feet long. The metaphor is obvious: You are limited by how you see the world.

If you desire a goal that is possible but seems entirely out of reach right now, attempt it anyway. Don't be afraid of failure. Missing the mark and trying again is part of the process. Be afraid of the fear itself, for it may be the thing that's holding you back.

We choose our own limits in life. Many times, the limited thinking we practice is self-imposed. But you can be and do so much more than you believe is possible. It's amazing what can be accomplished if we only crash through the barriers that are stopping us. Rethink the choices and decisions that may be getting in your way. There are no limits, except the ones we put on ourselves.

When I first posed this idea on Facebook, my fans let me know I was operating from a place of limited thinking! To make the point that your goals should be reasonable for you, I made the comment that "If you're five feet tall, chances are you won't be a professional basketball player." What happened next? One of my readers, Nas Cruz, replied, "Hey, I'm 5'6" and I'm a former professional European and NCAA Division I basketball player. Impossible is nothing!" Just because your goal seems daunting, that's no reason not to try!

As the author Mignon McLaughlin wrote, "Learning too soon our limitations, we never learn our powers." So knock the "t" off of "can't!" Don't think that you are going to become great, think that you are great now. Don't think that you will begin to act in a great way in the future, begin now!

Keep at it!

> *Today's mighty oak tree is just yesterday's nut that held its ground.*
> —Anonymous

Have you noticed that when you plant something in the garden, it takes time to grow? We are like a garden in that regard. There is no immediate gratification. Flowers do not bloom instantly; they open to perfection slowly in the sun. This may be a disheartening fact, but it should not be a discouraging one. Efforts always yield results even if they are not always immediately apparent.

Don't be in a hurry to reach your goals or become overwhelmed by how far you have left to go. Take things one step at a time, and have patience. The biggest mistake you can make is to give up.

Too often people with so much potential end up below par. On the flip side, those less able win the race simply because they stuck with it. Whether you're playing guitar, trying to lose weight, training for the marathon or finishing up your education, stick with it to reach the finish line.

Success comes to those who want it the most and who focus their energy on reaching their goal. It takes patience and discipline. Rome wasn't built in a day.

If you're frustrated and feel like throwing in the towel today, try reading a biography of a person who has been successful in life. You may be shocked to learn what they went through before reaching their goal.

Be persistent. You will reach your goal, too!

Some thoughts on failure

Avoiding failure is perpetuated at school and into our days of adulthood. We are encouraged to win at all costs and labeled as losers if we fail. This teaching makes us think that not trying at all is better than trying and failing. Not so! If I fail at something (and I have many times), I try again until I get it right.

If you believe you are a failure just because you've failed at something, then that means everyone in the world is a failure. The Beatles were turned down by Decca Records. Look what happened to them! Michael Jordan was cut from his high school basketball team. If they had given up after their first rejections, we would never have experienced their creative genius!

Failure is neutral—not good, not bad, just part of life. Don't hold yourself back. Don't let a failure, perceived or real, keep you from trying something else. Keep at it, whatever you are trying to achieve today!

Truth is, if you don't fail at something, then you never grow. Often it's the initial failures that help us evolve into the success for which we strive. How many entrepreneurs have said in interviews that, when they were getting started, they learned much more about their industry, their craft and their company from their mistakes than from their successes? Failing can be educational!

Look at what you have done, not at what you haven't been able to do. You may have accomplished a lot, and yet you let yourself become frustrated by giving attention to the things you didn't accomplish. Give yourself a little credit. If you are trying to reach a goal that requires consistent discipline and you backslide, don't be too hard on yourself. If you have a bad day, forget about it and begin again. Congratulate yourself for all the good days you had before.

If you're disappointed because you didn't get an outcome that you wanted, ask yourself: Were you really prepared for it? Remember, you must believe you are truly worthy of what you are expecting. Just as you would prepare for a dinner party by cooking in advance, you should prepare for all the positive outcomes you desire by expecting them to happen. Make plans, look forward, and all that you want will come to pass. If you didn't do this the first time, do it now and stay the course!

There are so many talented, educated people out there who are unsuccessful. It's not because they're not qualified. It's because they have the wrong mindset. Without the proper outlook and self-confidence, even the best credentials in the world will not help you succeed. Being successful includes seeing yourself as successful. If you can't see it, you may lose the direction needed to follow your goals and ultimately reach them. This includes being able to keep moving ahead, even when rejected one or many times. Keep a positive attitude, remember your strengths, see yourself as a winner and you surely will be!

No failure—or success, for that matter—is necessarily final. No matter how many times you have failed in the past, remember that your past does not dictate your future. If you tried to make a positive change before and couldn't achieve it, keep trying again and again. With determination, anything is possible.

SUE SAYS

We all have the capability, imagination, and foundation to achieve extraordinary results and be the outstanding person we were meant to be. The secret lies in having a clear goal, listening to our inner voice, taking continuous small steps, acting despite fear, adjusting as we proceed, and not giving up when things get tough.

The price of success

If you want to take yourself to the next level, you must be willing to pay the price that greatness requires. You must be determined to work harder than everyone you know. There's no shortcut. Hard work is and always will be the key to success. It's not just about looks or talent; there are plenty of attractive, talented people who are not successful.

To be your best, you must invest all you are in becoming all you wish to be.

It will take courage, self-control and determination to reach your goal. No matter what the battle, if you really want to win, there's no easy path to glory, there's no road to fame. Life, however we may view it, is no simple board game. Its best prizes call for fighting, endurance and grit. Don't give up!

Handling ups and downs

We all get discouraged from time to time. Even I occasionally feel that no matter what I do, it's somehow not worthwhile. Sometimes I take two steps forward, only to have something happen to bring me back three steps. The challenge is to accept that feeling as a temporary state that in no way defines who we are or what we're able to accomplish. If we're able to accept that feeling, we gain our vigor back and our discouragement will quickly become encouragement. We are always going to have negative experiences that try to bring us down, but if we keep ourselves focused on the positive, these discouraging experiences will fade away as quickly as they appeared.

In life, there will always be upturns and downturns. Success is typically a long road that requires daily work to make it a reality. If you really want to achieve your goal, simply do not give up. It will happen. Don't expect it to happen overnight, but expect it to happen. Powerful results come from taking baby steps, day after day, until you reach your goal.

And along the way, celebrate *all* of your accomplishments, big and small. Achievement is not always about winning awards or getting to the finish line first. As proud as I am that I achieved my goal of writing this book, I am also proud of the time I created an amazing mixed berry cobbler that drew smiles from my family. Take note of all of your successes, for sometimes it's the little ones that count the most!

4

Here's to Your Health:
Exercise and Eating Right

When it comes to eating right and exercising, there is no "I'll start tomorrow." Tomorrow is disease.

—V.L. Allineare

Think of your body as your house. If it had a weak foundation (and you knew it), would you feel comfortable living in that house? How are your walls, floors, plumbing, electrical, roof and ceiling? Notice I didn't ask about your paint. That's not important if the walls are falling down and the lights aren't working. Your "paint"—your skin—will look great if you are healthy from the inside.

Houses can be repaired and improved, and so can your health. It takes effort and discipline, but it can be done!

Exercising and eating right are essential to your well-being and your longevity. They ward off a host of illnesses and keep your body operating at peak performance. I'm really an advocate for both, so this chapter is written with a great deal of passion. I live this advice every day!

Because most of my clients who seek help with eating right and exercising are ultimately trying to lose weight, I have written this chapter mostly from a weight-loss point of view. But you can also use these tips simply to improve your overall health, or to fine-tune the efforts you're already making in these areas.

All good things in life take time, so don't go for the quick fix! Change your exercise and food habits a little at a time. It may take months, maybe even a year, but when you do see results, they'll last a lifetime. Exercise regularly and eat moderately, and you'll never have to diet again!

SUE SAYS

Learning to love your body is a process. It's like using a potter's wheel. You mold the clay around and around until your creation is perfectly formed. Like the gradual layering of the clay around the wheel, you can create a positive, life-affirming relationship with the body you live in. Loving your body can be hard, but it is worth every ounce of effort you put into it!

Exercise

Movement is a medicine for creating change in a person's physical, emotional and mental states.

— Carol Welch

If you're like many people, your day consists of commuting a half hour or more to work, sitting at a desk for six or seven hours and then commuting home. Your typical evening consists of four hours of watching television before turning in. If this describes you, you may be paying the price—physically, mentally and emotionally—for living a sit-down life. Bodies are designed to move, and when they don't, they stop being efficient.

That's why regular exercise is as much a necessity in life as bathing and brushing your teeth.

I recommend (and I do) exercise every day. But if you can't do it every day, at least do some sort of aerobic activity (something that causes your heart rate to go up) three days a week for a minimum of 30 minutes. Just 30 minutes will decrease stress, burn calories and amp up your metabolism so that you continue to burn calories several hours after you work out.

It's absolutely okay to start small!
Physical activity comes in all forms. How you exercise is completely up to you. There are many ways to do it right.

Setting extreme exercise and change-of-lifestyle goals (as we often do for our New Year resolutions) will most likely guarantee failure. Instead, set goals that are more realistic. You can take little steps and still see big results—it just takes time. Baby steps lead to success!

Delete the words "try" and "should" from your vocabulary. If your goal is to start exercising, here are the most powerful, action-oriented words you can use: "I *will* start exercising, and I *will* begin by [set your date]." By writing this down by hand on paper, you solidify your goal even more. Words of action such as "will" "can" and "must" leave no room for excuses.

If you're not sticking to any exercise regimen right now, make it easier. Try exercising for five minutes in any way you want. That's it. Just five minutes a day may not be a lot, but you're creating the exercise habit and improving your health. Do this for a month and you now have such a solid exercise habit that you miss it if you skip a day. The self-satisfaction will encourage you to continue and add the extra time needed for better results.

Next time you clean your house, pay attention to how much you're moving. You're probably getting in some exercise! I thought I was in good shape until I decided to give my house a thorough cleaning. It almost made me rethink my workout routine. Being on my hands and knees cleaning floors must be great exercise since I was totally winded after. Housecleaners are worth every penny they make. What a job!

In the same vein, why not turn mundane chores into a chance to burn calories? When I brush my teeth, I do squats and lunges. Two times a day equals 20 to 40 squats! When putting away laundry, I have to run downstairs to retrieve each load; I end up working up a sweat. Next time you do the floors, put on some music and vacuum, sweep or mop to the beat. You can dance a little as you stir a pot or load the dishwasher.

My kitchen is on two levels, and I often use the step down to the lower part as an opportunity to exercise. While the TV is on, I'll do a mini round of step aerobics right there in the kitchen. Be creative! Exercise doesn't have to be a marathon session, and it can be done practically anywhere. Doctors recommend at least 30 minutes of exercise every day, but those minutes don't have to be consecutive. Ten minutes here and ten minutes there and before you know it, you've reached or passed the 30-minute mark. Start thinking about it this way, and you'll begin to see the exercise opportunities around you.

Sometimes, sneaking in extra exercise is simply a matter of doing things a little differently. The next time you drive, park a few blocks from your destination. Parking just five minutes away can add an hour of exercise per week. At shopping malls, park at the far end of the lot. If you take public transportation, get off a few stops earlier and walk the rest of the way.

In many public places, such as hospitals and government office buildings, signs encourage people to use the stairs instead of the elevators. Great idea! Taking the stairs burns about seven calories per minute. Climbing a flight of stairs is great, heart-healthy exercise. I challenge you to use stairs today, at least once, instead of an elevator

Discipline is hard. It takes commitment and a "can do" attitude. Too many barriers leave us discouraged. They shouldn't! Small changes toward getting more exercise will ultimately add up to a healthier, slimmer, happier you!

SUE SAYS

Remember, you can't make a difference by doing good only once in a while. You have to form good habits and practice them day in and day out. Living a healthy lifestyle will only deprive you of illness, low energy and depression.

Dancing is a great workout!

My "go to" exercise on a daily basis is dancing! The time goes by quickly, and you don't even realize the amount of calories you're burning. It has to be one of the best cardiovascular exercises there is!

According to the American Heart Association, dancing a ballroom dance three times a week for eight weeks is just as effective for improving cardiopulmonary function as exercising on a treadmill. And dancing can give you a great mind-body workout, too. Researchers are learning that regular physical activity in general helps keep your body, including your brain, healthy. Exercise increases the level of brain chemicals that encourage nerve cells to grow. Doing more complex dances, such as the tango, requires you to remember steps and sequences, which boosts brain power by improving memory skills.

But you don't have to learn a formal style of dance to make it work. You don't even need a partner. Just dance around the house to any music you like. It really helps relieve the stress of the day!

Sometimes it's fun dancing when no one else is around! There's a certain freedom in it. And I can't emphasize enough what a great workout it is!

You don't need a gym membership or any equipment, just something that plays music. Dance to whatever music moves you. Get a CD compilation of upbeat songs from the decade you love most. Or go online to a free website such as www.musicchoice.com and play your favorite channel. I dance every day to the Dance/Electronica channel on this site. Though I may be a woman of a certain age, it doesn't stop me from dancing for an hour to the likes of Beyoncé or Lady Gaga! I just choose my music and dance my heart out.

Try it, even for a few minutes. Your heart is begging you! And you'll be surprised how *great* you'll feel afterward.

Other fun ways to move your body

Remember the games you played as a child—skipping, jumping rope, hopscotch? Back then, exercise didn't seem like a chore! As a kid, you'd run around at recess or take your bike for a spin just for fun. Bring that sense of play back to your workouts and you'll be more likely to get moving, stick with it and see results.

You can even do the same movements! Skip around the house. Make believe you're playing hopscotch in your living room. Jumping rope is a phenomenal workout. Jump for ten minutes, and you'll burn as many calories as you would in 45 minutes of swimming! As an adult, I decided to start hula hooping again. I used to be great at it when I was a kid, and it's serious exercise. Who knew back then?

If you think outside the box and do something you enjoy, you'll get healthy and have a great time doing it. I have a small exercise trampoline that is a ton of fun. It's amazing to jump, dance, anything! I love it. It's a great aerobic workout. (You can get one for yourself at www.urbanrebounder.com.)

Don't let the fear of being ridiculed stop you. Be yourself. If you're happy doing the hula hoop as exercise, don't listen if people laugh or make fun of you. If it works for you, GO FOR IT. Exercise is like personal style: Do what feels right for you. We don't need everyone looking exactly the same, and you don't have to exercise in precisely the same way as anyone else.

When I first starting aerobic boxing and kickboxing for exercise years ago, my biggest critics were my three young sons. I sparred in the basement with a bag, not really knowing what I was doing, and they laughed at me and told me I looked stupid. It didn't stop me, and to this day, they still make fun of me if they happen to see me. I don't care.

If you try something new and fumble at it, just laugh at yourself and note that at least you tried it. If you look around a gym, there are many people who work out in their own unique way. Whatever works! They are not intimidated nor do they care what others think. Who's the winner? The one who may look funny but still exercises, or the one who is self-conscious and doesn't exercise?

Starting an exercise routine is the easy part. Sticking to it is the challenge! Find something you enjoy. If you hate to run, don't take up jogging or using a treadmill; you'll eventually lose interest. Experiment until you find the activities you look forward to. I've been sparring with that boxing bag in my basement, an hour at a time, for almost twenty years! I just enjoy it. Like what you do and you'll stay with it.

Use your mental powers for good, not evil

Your mind is a powerful partner in your quest to get in or stay in shape. It can also be a formidable foe, so use it the right way—to assist you in your efforts and boost your motivation.

Shift your thinking from couch potato mentality to thinking like an athlete. How do I need to move today? Where can I move my body today? What will I wear to feel comfortable? This may sound like a big challenge, but it's not as big a leap as you think. Committing to a fitness routine begins in your head, and there really is no such thing as lack of time if you really want to do it. Make the time to exercise. Do you really need to watch four hours of TV each night? If you can't give up your shows, you can ride an exercise bike or use a treadmill while you watch. Set an example for your kids, your spouse, your friends.

Visualization is another very important aspect of success. When you visualize, you rehearse how a problem can be solved, how a goal may be achieved or what rewards await you when you finish your task. This works really well for helping you stick with your exercise program.

If you want to get in shape, find a picture of a time when you liked the way you looked. Study it daily and display it in a prominent place—on the fridge or bathroom mirror. (If anyone around you is critical, just keep your picture in a private place such as a folder.) Look at it before you go to sleep and when you awaken. By doing so, you're visualizing your future, and the end result will be a healthier you!

Don't have a photo like that? You can actually create a picture of yourself at your ideal weight. Go to www.WeightMirror.com. Upload a picture of yourself, plug in your stats and you can see yourself as slim as you like! (The site is free, so go for it.)

To help you lose weight, visualize how you'll feel with your new body. What new clothes will you buy? What experiences will you try that you may be too self-conscious to try right now? (By the way, I don't believe in holding back your life until you're the right weight. Be sure to try new things and have adventures regardless of where you are in your journey.)

Visualization can also help with motivation. Occasionally I don't sleep well, and the next day I may have a little trouble starting my daily workout. To overcome this, I think about all the good things my exercise regimen does for my mood, my body and even my complexion! That's enough to get me up and boxing, rowing or dancing on my trampoline.

Another good way to approach losing weight is to write up a

weight-loss contract for yourself. Put in all the necessary steps you'll need to do to achieve your goal and sign it.

Mind games to avoid

Your mind can help you reach your health improvement goals—but it can also prevent you from getting there.

Don't use your mind to create excuses for not exercising or eating right. Excuses are harmful. They prevent you from succeeding. Telling yourself that you'll never lose weight because of your genes, your lack of time, your lack of support, and so on,will create a self-fulfilling prophecy. Resolve to start being responsible today. Don't find an excuse, find a way! If you want something badly enough, you will always find a way!

Don't hang up a picture of a thin model as motivation, or buy an outfit three sizes too small. They won't help, and they may make you feel worse about yourself. Use that mental energy to plan short-term goals, like eating a healthier dinner, or find a way to sneak in an extra 30 minutes of exercise in a fun way!

Whatever you do, don't compare yourself to others. Everyone works out and loses weight according to his or her own body structure. Be kind to yourself. That person on the treadmill next to you might be thinner than you, but you never know what health problems (or life problems) he or she might be enduring right now.

Who says you need a gym to get in shape?

If you have legs and arms, you have all the equipment needed to exercise! Walk! You already know how to do it and it's free. Ride a bike, garden, do yoga, jump rope, take an inexpensive exercise class at the Y! There are so many simple exercise options available that you just don't have any excuses. Your body and mind will thank you in a myriad of ways.

To improve your health or to lose weight, don't feel pressured to sign a contract with a gym. You'll probably end up paying without going or quitting outright within a few months. There are many other ways to get the same results.

If you're looking for a great way to work out without leaving home, I strongly recommend the Wii Fit Plus™ by Nintendo! The program has dozens of activities that involve aerobics, yoga, strength training and balancing, along with fun activities such as skateboarding and kung fu, plus customizable targeted exercises! The system will weigh you, determine your body mass index (BMI) and keep track of your progress on a daily basis. It can also record up to eight different profiles, so the whole family can use it. I put someone I know on this regimen and he lost 30 pounds! (Go to www.wiifit.com to learn more.) Best of all, Wii is just fun!

When you travel, use the complimentary workout area or pool at your hotel. If there isn't one or it's not open, you can still work out in your room using a chair or the bed to do pushups and the hallway to do lunges. If you're fortunate enough to be traveling to the beach, consider doing 30 minutes of one of these seaside activities in order to burn calories: building a sandcastle (burns 89 calories); running on the sand (321); swimming in the ocean (286); or tossing a Frisbee (71).

We all know that running or weightlifting will burn calories. But many activities we do every day burn amounts of calories similar to exercise routines. For instance, did you know that one hour on a stationary bike with moderate effort will burn as many calories as shoveling snow, chopping wood or moving furniture for the same amount of time? Making the bed can burn around 140 calories. Grocery shopping can burn up 200 to 300 calories.

It's no wonder that people who work on farms live longer than the average person. Milking a cow for an hour burns 259 calories; baling hay, 689!

Here are some activities that are outside normal exercise routines, and the approximate amount of calories you will burn if you do them for one hour. (This is adapted from the American College of Sports Medicine's *Resource Manual for Guidelines for Exercise Training and Prescription*.)

Boxing (punching a heavy bag): 400 to 500 calories
Bowling: 159 to 211 calories
Football (touch or flag): 562 to 689 calories
Golf (carrying clubs): 387 to 474 calories
Handball: 844 to 1,034 calories
Martial arts: 703 to 862 calories
Jumping rope (moderate effort): 700 to 862 calories
Backpacking: 492 to 603 calories
Belly dancing: 500 calories
Gardening: 300 to 400 calories

The bottom line: Find something you enjoy doing. If what you're doing is fun, you'll do it more often. You never have to get stuck in a rut. If you don't like the way you're working out, try something else! When the weather is warm, try walking, swimming, biking, kayaking, tennis. When the weather is cold, depending on where you live, try skating, skiing, hiking, mall walking, or just staying inside with your Wii. It's all out there for you!

Hey, is your car dirty? Forget the carwash. Do it yourself and burn almost 400 calories!

Housework is exercise! Vacuuming for 30 minutes burns about 90 calories; dusting for 30 minutes burns about 50 calories; and ironing for 30 minutes burns about 70 calories.

Just because you're working out, it doesn't mean you can't look great. Many shops offer stylish, lightweight workout gear for everything from lifting weights to doing Pilates to lounging at home. Target, for one, has a great selection and doesn't break the bank!

SUE SAYS

You are actually burning calories while you're reading this. If you are standing while you're reading this, you will burn even more calories. In fact, if you are standing and pacing around, you'll burn even more calories!

The benefits of working out

I can't stress enough how important it is to have a workout regimen. Not just once in a while—I mean having a set time every day so that it becomes as much a part of your routine as brushing your teeth and showering! Sure, you've probably heard it all your life: "Being a couch potato is bad and working out is good." But has anyone ever told you what you stand to gain? It's far more than making you look better physically. Working out has major benefits! Keep reading. This information may be the catalyst you need to change your daily routine.

Working out strengthens and boosts your immune system. It's a powerful natural immune cell stimulator, which means you're less likely to catch an infectious disease, such as a cold or stomach bug. Regular cardiovascular workouts (running, walking or biking) have been shown to lessen the occurrence of colds and flu. So, instead of worrying about catching the flu bug next winter, why not catch the workout bug? Just 30 minutes of exercise a day will build up both your immune system and your muscles! (Another tip for beating colds: I drink a mixture of Celestial Seasonings Red Zinger herbal tea mixed with pomegranate concentrate every day. It's filled with immune-boosting antioxidants.)

People who work out regularly have better memories and longer attention spans than people who are sedentary. Aerobic activity stimulates the portions of the brain that handle executive function, which is associated with better attention and keeping your goals in mind.

There are so many factors that cause stress in our lives. Between the troubled economy, natural disasters, and just plain everyday living, chronic stress can get out of control. Stress can be a good thing in certain situations, but if it becomes a way of life, it can take a terrible toll on your body. Some common side effects of stress are constant fatigue, insomnia, and muscle aches. We can't avoid the situations that cause stress, but we can do things to help alleviate it. One thing that really helps is taking time out every day to exercise. Any form of exercise has a powerful effect on lowering stress. Listen to some uplifting music while you exercise and it's virtually impossible to think stressful thoughts. You may be saying that your life is too busy to find the time to do this, but, believe me, if you really try, you will! After all, your health and your happiness are worth it!

Exercising reduces stress and anxiety by lessening electrical activity in tense muscles. Also, your body releases more endorphins for one-and-a-half to two hours after your workout, which boosts mood and promotes relaxation. Most times, when you're physically active, you have more motivation to eat healthy . . . and eating healthy also reduces stress.

Regular exercise can increase sexual drive and satisfaction. Physical endurance and muscle tone improve sexual function by jump-starting the sympathetic nervous system, which increases blood flow to the genital area. Plus, when you feel healthy, you feel sexier.

Many potential deadly diseases, such as high blood pressure, heart disease, osteoporosis, obesity, high cholesterol, cancer, stroke and even arthritis may be staved off by inserting a daily one-hour exercise routine into your life. Daily exercise can decrease your heart rate by more than three million beats per year!

For those of us over 40, you'll be happy to know that working out, in addition to improving muscle tone and increasing flexibility, also brings more oxygen and nutrients to the skin so that it's firmer and better nourished. You keep more of that youthful glow. Even better—exercise has been proven to help slow the aging process. All good reasons to get those 30 minutes in each day! Don't know about you, but as far as I'm concerned, if I can look and feel younger, bring it on!

Putting yourself on a daily exercise regimen will boost your confidence. When do you feel better about yourself: When you're sitting on the couch eating a bag of chips, or when you've just completed some physical activity? When you're out of shape and begin working out, seeing the difference in your muscle tone and how your clothes look on you is a huge motivator for sticking to a daily exercise routine.

A big reason for not working out is the excuse that you're too tired, either in the morning when you wake up, or in the evening after working all day. Even if you feel tired, make the effort to exercise. You'll be surprised how energized you would feel afterward. People who work out regularly have more energy and stamina with which to tackle daily activities than non-exercisers. Work out regularly and you'll notice how much easier ordinary activities, like carrying in grocery bags or mopping the floor, become.

Regular exercise is linked to improved sleep. Studies have shown that working out three or four times a week for at least 30 minutes helps you sleep better. (I suggest working out in the morning or afternoon, rather than near bedtime. Working out too close to your bedtime may leave you too energized to sleep.)

Working out actually lessens the tendency to overeat. Being idle causes boredom, which in turn makes us more likely to hit the refrigerator and cupboards looking for that snack we don't really need. Once you've worked out, you'll find you need less junk food because the endorphins from working out will sustain the part of your brain that's looking for pleasure from eating (even when you're not hungry). Exercise also generally suppresses your appetite a bit, so you're not as hungry at meal time.

If you suffer from stress, incorporate a stress-killing exercise into your routine. I swear by kickboxing (really, any boxing). It only takes a few minutes for that wonderful endorphin release to kick in. And it's also great for boosting flexibility. What stress-busting exercise can you turn to when things are getting to you?

If the benefits of just 30 minutes of exercise a day aren't enough to convince you to start a routine, then do it for someone who loves you: your spouse, your children, your parents. You owe it to yourself and to them to be the best you can be!

SUE SAYS

An unhealthy lifestyle leads to an unhappy life. Feeling healthy and looking healthy leads to a happier life. This is your one and only life, and your body is your sacred garment. Please take care of it!

Be safe, however you move your body

Keep these tips in mind as you look for ways to build your exercise program:

Hydrate. Always drink water when you exercise. Staying hydrated will keep your body functioning optimally and you feeling good. Just stay away from high-calorie sugared sodas and drinks.

Stretch. Don't start out cold. Give your arms and legs a little warm-up time before you begin your workout.

After my workout, I have a small serving of protein. It's satisfying, helps balance blood sugar levels and gives my muscles fuel for repair.

If you lift heavy weights, rest between sets to give your body time to recover. Try not to work the same muscle group two days in a row. Muscles grow with rest.

Summer is a great time to get outdoors and walk, bike, jog, swim—anything that gets you moving. However, when the temperature rises above 85, exercise can get risky. And if it's humid where you are, be careful even at lower temperatures. (Higher humidity can make it feel hotter since your body cannot cool off as efficiently by sweating.) Being too warm puts you at greater risk for illness. If you begin to feel any hint of nausea, dizziness, cramps or a headache, stop what you're doing, get something to drink and go inside to cool off.

Finally, getting a good night's sleep is just as important as exercise. In your deepest sleep, your body produces human growth hormone, which stimulates tissue repair in your muscles and tendons. And recent studies have linked lack of sleep to weight gain. Do your body a favor and get the sleep you need (seven to nine hours a night)!

Eating Right

Eating right is part of your well-being. It shows in the clarity of your skin, in your energy level. While we eat primarily for fuel, what we eat has a big impact on our health and our appearance. And eating, for most of us, is a real pleasure.

This section, like the previous section on exercise, is geared toward those seeking weight loss, but the information really applies to anyone looking to eat healthier or seeking peace in his or her relationship with food.

Losing weight (or simply eating better) really starts with thinking differently. My philosophy involves education, awareness and consistency.

Education: Realize that you have plenty of options, and the choice between them ultimately is yours.

Awareness: Ask yourself "What am I doing?" And slow down long enough to get the true answer.

Consistency: Do the right thing more often than the wrong thing.

Diets in general don't work in the long run. If you change your behavior temporarily, you will see temporary results. Go back to what you were doing, and you'll go back to the old results, too.

Instead, I advise making small changes for life. These can be as simple as watching your portion sizes, omitting sugary drinks and exercising regularly. Make the right small changes for life, and I promise, you will see the results you want.

I think a big reason people have issues with overeating is because from early childhood, food has been used as either a reward (if you do your homework, we'll go out for ice cream) or a punishment (no dessert because you didn't behave at dinner). We were trained that food has some kind of magical power beyond being nutrition to sustain us. Think about the commercials on television that urge you: "Indulge," "Reward Yourself," "You Deserve a Break Today." These are all messages about rewarding yourself with high-calorie, unhealthy "gifts." We pacify ourselves in adulthood with the same things our parents rewarded us with in childhood: food, especially sweet foods and salty snack foods. By rewarding yourself with high-calorie, low-nutrition treats, you only make yourself feel worse in the long run. Try other rewards. Here's one I often suggest: Take the money you would spend on expensive ice cream snacks and put it in a vacation fund every time you choose a healthy alternative. Yes, indulging from time to time is fun and even necessary, but catch yourself if you find that you are using food as a constant reward.

Sometimes your small changes must begin with ending the self-sabotaging habits that you've fallen into over time. A bad habit is simply an unconscious action that's become so routine that not doing it is now very difficult. Do you eat mindlessly in front of the television? Do you literally inhale your food because you need to be somewhere else very soon? You're not alone! Most of the time bad eating habits arise from convenience, the need for speed, stress relief and, to put it bluntly, lack of discipline. I will share some tips on overcoming the not-so-great habits that have become ingrained in your eating.

For the most part, in life you get what you believe you deserve. You've heard of a self-fulfilling prophecy? If you keep telling yourself that you won't get a job because the economy is lousy, or you won't lose weight because you have bad genes, you won't. Anything worth achieving is worth working for. Just wishing for something to happen is not going to make it happen. The fact is, in order to achieve success, you need direction, discipline, perseverance and the attitude that you can make it happen!

Childhood obesity is now the #1 health problem for our kids! We must act now to help them learn to make good choices that will follow them into adulthood. Otherwise, we're looking at a new generation filled with heart disease, diabetes and high blood pressure. Show your kids you love them by tossing the junk food and stocking your pantry and refrigerator with healthy snacks—fruits, veggies and low-fat options. And be a good role model: exercise regularly as an example, and get them involved in moving, too!

Eating and losing weight

There are good reasons why weight loss is a $30 billion industry. First, it's confusing. One day, we're told to avoid fats and only eat carbs. The next day, we're told to avoid carbs and eat fats! Second, there are so many gimmicks out there. Television is filled with infomercials touting the newest line of abs-crunching, miracle-working machines. Finally, we live in an era of instant gratification, with quick-fix diet plans that promise to drop three dress sizes in one month! But quick weight-loss programs rarely produce long-term effects. Miracle and starvation diets are unbalanced and unhealthy, and unless you have amazing discipline, you'll eventually return to your old habits. The weight will come back quickly.

Here's the truth: In general, long-term weight loss requires the right combination of good nutrition, aerobic exercise and building muscle. And long-term maintenance requires developing a healthy routine that will stay with you the rest of your life.

Rather than spending money to lose weight, first use your common sense. Tap into your genuine desire to get healthy. Read up on nutrition and exercise and start making the small changes that will add to big improvements.

Start with portion control. Oversized portions are probably the single biggest cause of weight gain. Restaurants brag about how huge their portions are. The portion size for many prepared and frozen foods are also very large—they're really two portions, but are you really going to eat just half?

Instead of drastically cutting your portions, reduce them by just a bit. (This works better if you also get smaller dinner plates and bowls.) Spend a little time in your kitchen getting a better idea of what a sensible portion is. A standard portion of cooked pasta, for instance, is one cup, which works out to about 200 calories. Cook up some pasta and measure out how much is in a cup. I bet you've been eating a lot more than that and not realizing how many calories you were taking in. Practice with some other foods as well to get a better handle on portion sizes.

If you want to lose weight, remember that one pound of body fat is the equivalent of about 3,500 calories. Eat 3,500 more calories than you use over the course of two weeks, and you will gain a pound, because you're adding an extra 250 calories a day. But cut 250 calories from your diet each day and you'll lose a pound in about two weeks. A good way to start lowering your calorie intake is to just cut your portion size. Do this regularly for a few weeks and soon a bigger portion size will look enormous to you.

Look for foods that fill you up without a lot of extra calories. A baked potato (100 calories) is far more satisfying than 20 potato chips which, at 115 calories, will add up very quickly. The chips are full of added fat and salt and missing all the good nutrition, like fiber and potassium, found in a baked potato. (See "Tips, tricks and substitutions" later in this chapter for more smart swaps like this one.)

Whatever you do, don't skip meals. When you want to lose weight, it may be tempting to starve yourself. But eating small amounts of food frequently can help you maintain a healthy, balanced calorie intake—and healthy blood sugar levels—throughout the day.

Once you've cut your calories, pair it with consistent exercise and you'll be on your way.

Are you sabotaging your healthy eating?

Do you feel that you eat well but still can't seem to make the extra weight budge? This is where a little education and awareness might help you break through your impasse.

Let's say that you're a big believer in salads. You eat a salad almost every day at lunch, so why is your weight creeping up? Sure, salad is healthy, but not the extras! Much of what is offered at the typical salad bar is processed food, packed with calories along with unwholesome preservatives and nitrates. Bacon bits are full of saturated fats and sodium. Croutons are usually derived from refined flour, containing little in terms of vitamins or nutrients. Salad dressings are often filled with calories, including calories from added sugar. The solution is easy: Choose chicken or turkey and raw veggies for your toppings. Dip veggies into the dressing instead of pouring it on top. Leave off the croutons and bacon bits. You'll save a lot of calories!

Bread is not the enemy. It's naturally low in fat, and if you exercise you'll easily burn the calories. It's what you put on the bread that counts! Skipping dressings on your sandwiches, such as mayonnaise, will save you at least 100 calories. Try regular or Dijon mustard instead. Both are full of flavor and are only 5 calories per serving.

Most of us rely on coffee first thing in the morning to wake us up. There are many health benefits attributed to regular coffee, but do we ever give a moment's thought to how many calories that innocent-looking latte could contain? Be careful: You could be downing 200 to 400 extra calories. And stay away from frappuccinos, as they can waste up to 500 calories! Take a Starbuck's grandé iced peppermint white chocolate mocha with whipped cream, for instance. That's about a third to a quarter of your daily calories in one 16-ounce cup. Instead, drink regular coffee (I use soy creamer instead of dairy).

Remember, never drink your calories. The average can of regular soda contains the equivalent of ten teaspoons of sugar. Some sugary soft drinks have 400 calories or more. A 16-ounce triple-thick shake at McDonald's is 565 calories. Always look at the label on bottled drinks, and don't overlook the serving size; just half a bottle can be 150 calories. Think about it: If you drink two to three drinks a day, that can add up to half of your entire day's calories! Instead, stick to water and unsweetened tea. Get your calories from more satisfying and nutritious foods.

Modifications and substitutions for what you currently eat can improve your health beyond weight loss. For example, did you know that, according to a study from the University of Minnesota, people who prefer their red meat very well done are 60 percent more likely to get pancreatic cancer than those who eat their meat rarer or eat no meat at all. Charred meat contains carcinogens, so trim all the burned portions before you indulge. Keep learning about healthy eating and it will serve you, no matter your weight!

How to overcome your bad eating habits

Bad habits come in many different forms. Some are physical: smoking, overeating, lack of exercise. Others are emotional: negative thinking, over-stressing, and so on. Whatever the bad habit is, you *can* break it. For each bad habit, there is a positive action step that will help you get rid of it. This isn't about occasional actions, it is about persevering *every day*. I'm not saying it will be easy. It takes discipline. At first, you'll probably want to revert back to your old, comfortable habits, bad as they are, but hang in there. Visualize yourself as the person who has already broken the bad habit(s). See yourself in a new future, one where you are the person you were meant to be. Stay close to others who also want to make positive changes and those that have been successful at it. Tell yourself every single day, "No matter what, I can do it."

None of us is immune to bad eating habits. We each have our specific weaknesses and triggers that cause us to go overboard. The first step is simply recognizing what your weakness is. Then, set a goal to change your habit and stick to it. Start slowly.

Have you trained yourself to go immediately to the refrigerator when you turn on the TV? Do you start to overeat when you're stressed? These are triggers that, once you're aware of them, you can control through mindfulness. Wear a rubber band around your wrist and every time you feel yourself reaching for that unhealthy snack, just snap the rubber band to remind yourself to pick another option.

Mindless eating in front of the TV is probably one of the most common bad eating habits. We've trained ourselves to equate watching television with eating. Many times, we're not even hungry! We just snack because it's what we're used to. The next time you turn on the TV, try not to eat anything. If you must snack, take a small portion with you to where you watch TV, and don't allow yourself to go back into the kitchen. A fruit, a bunch of grapes, or even a piece of gum will satisfy your need to chew without adding on the calories.

Another bad habit is being addicted to junk food. How can we resist its siren call? We're tempted by commercials promoting sugary cereals, pastries that melt in our mouths and potato chips that crunch with every bite. These snacks were originally designed to be addictive, and they sure turned out to be just that!

Well, the same people that came up with these snacks are now working to help our growing obesity problem by creating low-fat, low-calorie options. But remember, even though you can now get junk food that's low-fat and low-calorie . . . it's still junk food! So, eat in moderation. Junk food is engineered to trigger the pleasure and addiction centers of your brain, so first try to limit your consumption to a specific time—maybe only on the weekend. Midweek, replace your junk food cravings with healthy alternatives. Carrots make excellent snacks (I eat at least 20 carrot sticks a day). Also, apples and berries are sweet and filling. The idea is that you'll eventually break the addiction. And then you can choose whether to continue indulging on the weekends, or ultimately replace that junk food with something healthier or more satisfying. Just remember, you always have options!

Tips, tricks and substitutions

In no particular order:

Never skip meals. Eat at regular intervals so you don't get hungry (and go overboard) in between. Breakfast is by far the most important meal, so if you tend to miss it in the rush of the morning routine, try bringing a protein bar or nutritional bar with you in the car or on the train. And the old story: Don't shop for groceries when you're hungry. You'll buy everything in sight.

Fill up before you face the real temptations. Clear, veggie-filled soups are great for filling you up so that you will eat less (stay away from creamed soups). You can slash 150 calories from your lunch or dinner by snacking on an apple right before your meal. The high fiber and water content fills you up, and it's a great way to get extra vitamins and minerals into your diet!

If you tend to reward yourself with food, find another reward such as buying yourself flowers or a new outfit. Take a bubble bath, read a magazine, go for a walk.

Don't eat right away if you get a hunger pang. Wait ten minutes and see if the urge passes. Or drink a glass of water, as you may simply be thirsty (sometimes thirst signals itself from the stomach, not the throat). Keep an apple or orange slice next to your bed to help stop you from getting up and hitting the refrigerator in the middle of the night.

Think water. Drink plenty of it. Replace your caffeinated beverages and diet sodas with plain water if you can. Eat water-rich foods to help shrink your waistline: cucumbers, tomatoes, melons, lettuce, oranges. You will feel fuller faster, thus saving you calories!

When you want to snack at home, skip the chips and dip and stick with plain popcorn. Instead of rich, high-calorie frozen desserts, try freezing red or green grapes; ten grapes have 60 calories and no fat! Having plenty of healthy snacks around will help you stay on track. If you don't see the high-calorie, high-fat snacks, you won't eat them, so get them out of your pantry!

Sugar tends to increase cravings, so skipping it may help your ability to withstand temptation. Sometimes brushing your teeth or chewing gum will stop a food craving. Not many foods taste good just after you've made your mouth minty fresh.

Slow down when you eat. Savor each bite. It takes the brain time to register a feeling of fullness. Slowing down will keep portions at a healthy size. Put your fork down between bites and focus on the conversation. When I have coffee with friends, I can make one biscotti last two hours!

Cheating: how to do it . . . and make peace with it
If you crave an occasional sweet, dessert or other treat that you enjoy, don't deprive yourself. Not letting yourself have it will only make that treat more and more desirable to you, and may derail you from the progress of all your other good work. Allow yourself to have it . . . but only a small bite or a quarter of a regular serving. Most foods taste best in the first few bites, so really pay attention as you eat it.

If you continue to desire one type of food again and again, see if there's a healthier substitute you can incorporate from time to time that will satis-fy your craving. My guilty pleasure is Trader Joe's Soy Creamy "ice cream." If you crave the taste of real ice cream, take my word for it—this is the best alternative! It comes in mango/vanilla gelato, cherry chocolate chip and chocolate. It's all-natural, vegan, lactose- and gluten-free. Each serving is only 2.5 grams of fat. (For store locations, go to www.traderjoes.com.)

Also, think about what you're getting out of your "cheat." For example, you could have a can of soda at 150 calories, or a café smoothie or latte at 300 calories. Or you could eat an apple and/or a serving of hummus with pita points for the same calorie content. In the end, which will satisfy you more at that moment? Eat the one you really want, but be aware that you always have options. The healthier options may actually be more appealing when you think about it!

For people who are trying to lose weight, the guilt that goes with cheat-ing can make things far worse than they are. There's nothing wrong with an occasional splurge. But our "all or nothing" thinking can sometimes make us throw all of our good habits out the window when we cheat just once. We beat ourselves up by not being perfect in our eating. Sometimes we feel so bad about ourselves, we cheat even more.

Rather than letting guilt or a temporary derailment undo or sabotage your progress, approach eating as if you were a student. There are two ways to do this: You can eat like an A student during the week, and do a little (I repeat, a little) C student splurging on the weekends. This way, you have something to look forward to. Or, you can eat like a B student all the time, so you won't run the risk of feeling deprived. Allow yourself to sample small tastes of your favorite foods all week long so that you stay on an even keel; just be sure you have them in moderation.

The student method will work as long as you average a B. It won't work if you go from being an A student during the week to a D student on the weekends! Gorging on high-calorie foods or eating everything in sight on Saturday and Sunday can negate your entire week's hard work. Aim for a B average all the time and you'll be most likely to succeed!

Eating out: making the best choices

We have so many choices now when it comes to dining out in restaurants or grabbing takeout, whether from a fast-food place or a favorite gourmet market. Sure, cooking in gives you more control over the calorie content of your food, but going out to eat is a pleasure and often a necessity after a tough day! Eating out can pack a calorie wallop, though.

If you're going out and know you'll be tempted to over-indulge, eat a small, healthy snack beforehand (an apple, or even a cup of coffee), which will lessen your appetite.

On the menu, look for the good (healthy) words, like steamed, broiled, roasted and poached. Steer clear of high-fat terms such as buttery, creamed, au gratin, sautéed, fried, crispy, marinated, in oil, basted and casserole. Anything pickled or smoked will pack a very high sodium content.

Always ask for dressings on the side. This includes salad dressings, gravies and any sauces that are listed on the menu.

If you're drinking, opt for wine or light beer instead of daiquiris or other frozen sugary drinks. One of these drinks can be as many calories as your main course!

Watch your portions. Almost every U.S. restaurant serves too much food. Huge portions are even a selling point for some restaurants, with patrons believing it all has to be eaten to get the full value of the price paid. Remember, you're a grown-up now and you never have to clean your plate. Eat half or one-third of what's on your plate, and you'll stay in control. (Box it up, and you'll have another meal ready to go.)

Here are some tips by type of restaurant (or meal choice):

Italian: Choose tomato-based sauces (marinara) instead of cream or pink sauces (Alfredo or vodka).

Indian: Choose tandoori dishes instead of curries with coconut and cream.

BBQ: Choose spice rub instead of thick, sugary sauces.

Pizza: Choose thin-crust with veggie toppings instead of pan pizza with meat toppings.

Asian: Choose sushi instead of stir-fry with sweet sauces and white rice

American: Choose roast chicken with roasted veggies instead of fried chicken with cheesy potatoes.

In addition to restaurants, we often "eat out" when we go to the movies. Here's the 411 on movie munchies: One medium popcorn is 690 calories. Nachos are 780 calories. A hot dog is 448 calories. A 3.5-oz. box of Gummi Bears is 390 calories. So your best bet is to eat before you go! Or, do what I do: Bring in your own unsalted, unbuttered organic popcorn!

Enjoying holidays without weight gain

Most holidays include special food or big meals as part of the ritual. When you're trying to lose weight or eat healthier, holiday eating can seem like a roadblock to your progress. But it doesn't have to be.

Take Halloween. You know what it means when you're stationed at your front door: A few pieces of chocolate before the doorbell rings. A few more in between the ghosts and goblins. Plenty of leftovers when the night is through. Halloween is fun, but it can wreak havoc for even the most diligent dieter. One mini-Milky Way leads to ten before you know it.

My advice for Halloween is moderation. I once managed to make a Three Musketeers bar last a whole week. I took one bite a day! If you really have to indulge, stick to gummy candy or lollipops, as they have fewer calories.

Halloween is the perfect excuse to treat yourself to the delicious goodies of the season instead of candy. For the best treat of all, look no further than your jack-o'-lantern. Make soup or a great pumpkin bread! Add pumpkin to your oatmeal. And don't forget about pumpkin seeds. They are delicious roasted in the oven! Pumpkin is loaded with nutrients, beta carotene, potassium and fiber. It's also fat-free and low in calories. And there's no better time to indulge than Halloween!

What about the most food-based holiday of them all—Thanksgiving? It's traditionally the big meal kickoff to the holiday season. Our forefathers celebrated the plentiful harvest with a huge meal. We carry on that tradition today by cooking up turkey, stuffing, green bean casserole, potatoes, cranberry sauce, gravies, pies, breads and more. If there's one day we tend to overindulge in comfort food, this is it! Believe it or not, an average Thanksgiving dinner consists of 4,600 calories and 230 grams of fat—and that's before second helpings!

Most Americans gain an average of one to three pounds between Thanksgiving and New Year's, and this weight gain usually is not lost over time. However, I firmly believe you can enjoy Thanksgiving without the weight gain. Really! There are ways to enjoy the holiday and whittle down that high-calorie meal to a more sensible (and still scrumptious) indulgence.

First, it's important to note that you shouldn't try to *lose* weight from Thanksgiving to New Year's. You'll just frustrate yourself. Focus instead on *maintaining* your current weight and not gaining. You can always focus on losing after all the parties and big meals. Believe me, you'll be so proud of yourself when January comes around and the scale is the same number as it was before the holidays.

So, how do you enjoy Thanksgiving without gaining weight?

Reserve at least 30 minutes Thanksgiving morning for some type of cardio exercise. Walking, dancing, jumping, running, skipping, whatever! Maybe you can get the family out for a quick game of touch football. This will rev up your metabolism.

Distance yourself from finger foods and high-fat appetizers. If you want to snack beforehand, stick to veggies. Or eat an apple before you arrive, which will curb your appetite so that you don't show up to the meal in starvation mode.

If there's salad before the meal, fill up on that with a low-fat dressing, and you'll eat less during dinner. (But skip the croutons. They're wasted calories.)

Turkey generally has little fat. White meat without skin is your best choice. Instead of drowning it in high-fat gravy, try seasonings for added flavor. If you must have gravy, be stingy. Use just enough to moisten it.

If you're cooking or bringing a side dish, make over your recipes to reduce fat and calories. Instead of using butter and cream in those mashed potatoes, try some chicken broth to moisten it. Swap the sweet potato casserole (filled with sugar and butter) for a simple baked sweet potato. Ditch the green bean casserole and substitute steamed green beans or veggies instead. If you must have bread, avoid butter and dip the crust in some olive oil. Use low-fat broth in your gravy. For your stuffing, use whole-grain bread and more veggies. In addition, cook the stuffing separately from the turkey to prevent soaking up extra fat from the turkey.

If the meal is buffet style, take smaller portions of the higher fat and calorie items and fill up on the turkey. Try filling a salad plate instead of a dinner plate—you'll feel like you're eating a lot even though you're not.

Limit yourself to one plateful of food. Eat slowly and enjoy every bite. Eating slowly will help you get full quicker. Pay more attention to the great conversation around you.

Wine is the best choice of alcohol beverage. Stay away from fruity, sweetened alcohol drinks, as they can add up to 300 or more calories per drink! As I always say, don't waste your calories on liquids! If you're not imbibing, stick to water.

Rather than drink eggnog, which is especially high in fat and calories, look online for great sugar-free eggnog-flavored recipes. You'd be amazed how a little rum or vanilla extract can make sugar-free vanilla pudding taste just like eggnog!

Oh, the desserts . . . pecan pie, pumpkin pie and the like. Don't deprive yourself. Just take a small helping. Your best choice is pumpkin pie. Tip: Eating the filling and leaving the pastry crust can save you hundreds of calories!

The bottom line: Portion control! I cannot emphasize this enough. Even if your meal consists of the highest fat and calorie items, you can minimize your weight gain by sticking to small tastings of each item.

All in all, enjoying Thanksgiving with family and friends doesn't mean depriving yourself of great food. It doesn't have to be all or nothing. It's just a matter of including healthier versions of traditional favorites, watching your portions and getting in some healthy movement!

What and how should I eat?

Choosing the right foods determines your performance, as what we put into our bodies has a profound effect on how we feel and how much energy we have.

Ideally, we should be eating six smaller meals per day instead of three large meals. When we eat giant meals, it just bogs our bodies down. Sticking with lighter foods and eating smaller portions throughout the day keeps us going strong and steady. Eating this way is especially important if you're not getting a normal level of exercise throughout the day. (I say, eat a light lunch and use the rest of your lunch hour to take a walk or stretch!)

I try to eat an antioxidant-rich diet. Certain foods are natural aging inhibitors: spinach, carrots, blueberries, cherries and virtually any deep-colored fruit or veggie infuse the body with chemicals that fight free radicals, which promote disease and aging. Sunflower and pumpkin seeds and most nuts (especially almonds and walnuts) are also great for overall health and well-being.

It's even more encouraging to eat the foods you love when you learn the health benefits they can pack. Raisins and prunes are considered beauty foods, great for dry skin and hair and weak nails. Grapefruit is low in calories and also contains pectin, which lowers cholesterol and fat. Miso, one of the primary ingredients in Asian cuisine, has been touted by doctors for its healing properties against such conditions as high cholesterol, high blood pressure, cancer, chronic pain and food allergies.

Coffee may do more than rev up your energy! According to the *Journal of Dermatology*, drinking one cup a day has been associated with a 5 percent lower chance of developing non-melanoma skin cancer over your lifetime, due to coffee's ability to destroy tumor-causing cells. Just choose regular coffee over lattes and frappuccinos, so that you don't save your skin but expand your waistline! Research also shows that coffee drinkers are less likely to have type 2 diabetes, Parkinson's disease, dementia, some kinds of cancer, strokes, and heart rhythm problems compared to people who don't drink coffee.

My recommendation is to cut out all dairy foods. But if you must eat dairy, I recommend using only organic products, with no artificial hormones or antibiotics added. The same goes for meat and poultry products. We encounter enough chemicals and pollutants in our environment. We certainly don't need more from our food!

Take your vitamins. Multivitamins combat stress, energize the body and help the immune system. A healthy inside will show as a radiant, healthy outside.

Drink your water. Enough water helps the body function properly. It keeps the immune system healthy and flushes out waste and toxins. I recommend at least six glasses a day of pure water, not just decaffeinated, unsweetened beverages.

You'll love this one. If you're trying to lose weight, eat some dark chocolate! In a study from Denmark, researchers gave 16 participants 100 grams of either dark or milk chocolate and then, two hours later, offered them a slice of pizza. Those who ate the dark chocolate ate 15 percent fewer calories than those who ate milk chocolate, and they were less interested in fatty, salty and sugary foods. Try a chocolate with 70 percent or more cocoa. You're welcome!

Reaching Your Goals

I strongly believe that the reason most New Year's resolutions aren't fulfilled is because they are no more than thoughts and promises. To really achieve a resolution, you need to do some active goal-setting When you define what you want and write out a plan, you're much more likely to follow through than if you just think about what you want to achieve.

Write down your goal:

Step 1: Your goal statement should always start with defining your goal. For instance, "To stop smoking" or "to exercise every day." Decide what you want, keep it simple and write it down.

Step 2: Write down the date to reach your goal.(This is not written in stone. You can adjust the date if necessary).

Step 3: List obstacles to reaching your goal. (For instance, you don't have enough time to exercise)

Step 4: After each obstacle, write down an action step you will take to overcome the particular obstacle. (you can set your alarm and get up an hour earlier)

Step 5: Set a weekly time to track your progress.

Active goal setting is the script, the roadmap and the magic wand. The script is your own story of your future that you have the privilege to write for yourself; the roadmap is the actual plan so that you will know how to get there; and the magic wand is your vision, your imagination, and your ability to make your own dreams come true!

Your body is like a potted plant. If it doesn't receive regular attention, it will deteriorate. If you want to, keep a potted plant on your desk or kitchen windowsill to remind yourself, as you water and feed it, that your health needs the same loving care!

Whatever your specific goal, remember that nothing happens overnight. If you're trying to lose those extra pounds, don't give up if you don't see immediate results. Start slow. Dance to one song. Order a baked potato instead of fries. Walk a flight of steps. Do small steps consistently and weight loss will eventually follow.

Always consider the way you look and feel and not on how much you weigh. Think in inches lost, not in pounds lost (muscle weighs more than fat).

Remember, you are a valuable commodity. Whoever is in your life— your spouse, your child, a friend—needs you. Be kind and gentle to yourself. Celebrate your accomplishments and any small success you achieve. Forgive yourself and accept the fact that no one is perfect. Choose to move forward instead of remaining stuck in the past or replaying a mistake you made over and over in your mind. If you want to lose weight or to become healthier, you can do it!

Remember when we were kids, we used to say to each other, "I dare you to . . . ." Well, today I am saying to you, "I dare you to be the most magnificent, eager, courageous person out there!"! I dare you to run that marathon, I dare you to write that book, I dare you to start your exercise regimen. I dare you to follow your dreams because they are attainable. I dare you to leave those negative people in your life in a cloud of dust, and learn from those who have succeeded. Are you going to accept the challenge?

5.
Beauty and Personal Style for You

This chapter is devoted to you being you—shaping the most beautiful you inside and out, and developing the personal style that's uniquely yours. It's about being the best *you*, not about being a carbon copy of someone else. And it's really about loving and respecting your wonderful self, rather than trying to please anyone else. There are many instances when we have to make a good impression. That means looking as good as you can as often as possible. People meet each other in the most unexpected places; and you never know when opportunity will knock!

You already know how important image is when you're interviewing for a job, when how you look and how you speak are just as important as what you say. Studies have shown that 65 percent of the conveyed message is nonverbal (gestures, physical appearance and attire). In a way, every day can be like a little job interview. The image you project by the way you look and dress is your personal web page to the public. Do you want them to click on you for answers, or continue to surf on?

By knowing yourself, and giving yourself every opportunity to let your beauty show and to dress just for you, you will already be well on your way to taking good care of yourself—and making a good impression to boot!

Being the Most Beautiful You

I could give many tips on how to look great each day, but the most important is: Beauty comes from within. I truly believe that the definition of beauty is being confident and comfortable in your own skin. It's about believing in yourself and living a life of integrity, character and self-respect. Show people that you're truly more than meets the eye, and you will be more beautiful and desirable than you'll ever know.

It's a fact that we're not getting any younger, even though I truly believe we can look younger than our age. I have been asked before whether I use Botox. I don't, but I find that question to be a compliment, believe it or not. People assume if you're over a certain age that you must be doing something artificial to enhance yourself. It's not always the case, although I respect people's choices to do so. For me, the thoughts, good habits and tips I'm about to share are what have helped me. I hope they help you, too!

Real beauty is all about inner beauty

Character contributes to beauty. It fortifies a woman as her youth fades. A mode of conduct, a standard of courage, discipline, fortitude and integrity can do a great deal to make a woman beautiful.
—Anonymous

Beauty is not in the face; beauty is a light in the heart.
—Kahlil Gibran

Beauty is an inside job. Believe it or not, *we get to choose* whether we are beautiful, by the energy that emanates from within us and showers out onto others. When we fully grasp the bounty and splendor that lives within our core, then our true beauty shines through. Nothing, not huge amounts of makeup, hairspray or even fabulous clothes, can compare to the glow of inner beauty.

Our magazines and media place so much importance on outer beauty but very little is said about inner beauty. We're all influenced by what we see and read, and it's sad that many of us feel ugly and overweight in comparison to those images. If we stopped to focus on our strengths within, and made goodness and enthusiasm our trademarks, that inner confidence would shine through as the real beauty! It's the purity within that out-shines the face. Real beauty is not what we see, it's who we are.

I've met many people who are the epitome of beauty on the outside but, after realizing that there's nothing behind that physical beauty, I've actually begun to see them as ugly. The opposite holds true as well. There are people not particularly beautiful on the outside whose personalities are such that one sees them as truly beautiful.

I have a friend who is extremely intelligent, with a scientific degree. He also does freelance photography. He truly is a man about town, photo-graphing events as diverse as the Coney Island Mermaid Parade, art gallery openings, charity events, and so on. There's never been a time I've seen him that he's not grinning from ear to ear. He truly loves life and loves people, and his beauty shines through to everyone. I always feel a little happier in his presence. This man is a great example of what I mean by inner beauty.

We all know that, eventually, and unfortunately, our outer beauty fades. But with proper cultivation, we can enhance and sustain our inner beauty. The good news is that it's never too late to start. Here are a few tips on being beautiful from within:

Begin each day with gratitude for what you have.

Always speak positively to yourself. Self-confidence is truly one of the keys to being beautiful. You are valuable and lovable. In fact, you are a masterpiece! Believe it. Repeat it to yourself daily.

Be charitable with your time or money by helping others. Aiding those in need allows your light from within to shine!

Present a positive self-image by appreciating your good points. Have you ever stopped to think about the power of your thoughts? If you're constantly putting yourself down by thinking you're not good-looking enough, this shows on the outside—no matter how beautiful you are. Learn to admire your good traits with the same energy you use to hate your faults.

Develop interests in people, music, literature and art. The world is truly a rich place filled with immense treasures and interesting people.

Be willing to let yourself develop your innate talents and gifts.

Remember, we all have beauty inside us. Cultivate and nourish it, and it will grow in abundance. Enjoy your life. Be kind to others. You are beautiful. Enough said!

A smile is your greatest beauty accessory

Are you a person who smiles easily? Or do you walk around with a serious expression, maybe even a frown? What impact do you think your facial expression has on others?

Try smiling. See how it makes you feel. I try to smile as much as I can and find people smile back. Frowning only brings negative energy.

Ongoing sadness or the blues can take its toll on our beauty, affecting our hair, skin and nails. But a positive attitude and a sound mind and body will help you glow. The way you feel about yourself reflects on the outside, especially in your facial expression. If you're feeling stressed and annoyed, it will show on your face no matter how much makeup you put on or how well you dress! On the other hand, if you're comfortable with yourself, you'll exude beauty from within, even without any adornment.

When you smile, even when upset, your brain receives signals that make you feel more positive. One study showed that Botox injections for frown lines helped the subjects' moods improve simply because they couldn't frown anymore. But don't run out and get Botox—just smile! You will always look great. It truly is the second best thing you can do with your lips!

Make your beauty sleep yield twice the benefits

We all know the importance of a good night's sleep. Most adults need an average of eight hours every night. Of course, there are people who can function without being drowsy on as little as six, or can't function at all without at least ten. You probably already have an idea of what number makes you feel your best.

However, knowing how much sleep you need and getting that amount on a regular basis can be challenging. With our job demands, busy schedules and active family lives, it's often hard to turn off and leave the worries of daily life behind when it's time to sleep. And when you're over-scheduled and need those extra waking hours, sleep gets sacrificed.

Getting the good sleep you need can benefit your beauty in two ways. First, you simply look healthier. Your skin glows, you lose those dark circles under your eyes and you feel better, which shows in your face and your demeanor. Second, before you go to bed, you can apply quality products to your skin that will have a better chance of penetrating deeply without the diminishing effects of the sun's rays. Do this, and your beauty sleep will work twice as hard for you!

Ideally, you'll want to get to bed before 11 p.m., as the body recovers and recharges itself most between 11 p.m. and 1 a.m. One thing all my friends and family know is not to call my house after 9 p.m., as I'm usually in bed!

What if you have trouble sleeping? Exercising early in the day helps you fall asleep faster and improve your sleep quality. If you can't work out in the morning, do it at least three hours before you go to bed. The reason is that exercise raises your body temperature, and it takes several hours for it to dip back. Your body needs this cooling down to fall asleep.

A rich, hearty dinner topped off with a slice of cake might seem like the perfect way to end the day, but it's smart not to eat a large meal within two hours of bed. Eat your dinner earlier in the evening, and avoid heavy, rich foods as bedtime snacks. On the other hand, a light snack before bed can help promote sleep. Turkey, which contains tryptophan, and a glass of warm milk can help calm the brain and allow you to sleep better. Or try some apple slices with peanut butter. Noshing like this before bedtime can keep you from waking with hunger pangs in the middle of the night, but won't over-stimulate your digestive system (which can keep you awake).

Visualize yourself as a baby being rocked in your cradle or in a stroller. This scenario can increase your sense of security, which can promote restful sleep. (I've actually tried this and it worked!)

Darkness helps to increase sleep quality. Even a little light can alter your normal sleep rhythm. If a sleep mask is too uncomfortable, consider ways to darken your window coverings.

As much as possible, avoid things that trigger worry or anxiety before bed. Try not to watch the news (which is always bad) and stay away from violent television shows. (This one's terribly hard for me, as I'm a news junkie!)

Try not to drink too much liquid before bed, to avoid frequent bathroom trips. Although alcohol may initially make you feel drowsy, it can interfere with sleep and cause frequent awakenings. Also, some people are sensitive to tyrosine, found in many red wines.

If none of these tips work for you, there's a sleep program available that works great without the use of any medication. It's called Calmistry for Sleep, and you can learn more about it at www.drkorwin.com/blog/calmistry-for-sleep. It really does help. If you have trouble getting restful sleep, try it!

In addition to the Calmistry for Sleep program, Dr. Korwin developed a drug-free anti-anxiety program for anxious dental patients called Calmistry. You can learn more about this at www.calmistry.com.

Now, getting back to our beauty sleep, *never* go to bed without washing your face. Nothing ages you more than leaving makeup and dirt to seep into your pores over night. In addition to washing your face, moisturizing is the gold standard of care.

What products should you apply? That depends on your skin type and your goals. I strongly believe in moisturizing heavily, especially before bedtime, and recommend using an antioxidant retinol moisturizer on your face and body at night. If you have dark circles and puffiness around your eyes, look for a product specifically designed to combat that. (If you tend to rub your eyes during the night, try an eye mask.)

My favorite brands for nighttime products are found in drugstores: Roc, L'Oreal, Olay and Neutrogena. All have "anti-aging" product lines that fight deep wrinkles. I also highly recommend a product found in natural markets called Unpetroleum, which is like a natural Vaseline without the petroleum. I use it to seal in my moisturizers.

If you sleep on two pillows, keeping your head elevated, this will prevent fluid from collecting around your eyes during the night and causing puffiness in the morning. But here's an important tip: Sleep on either a satin pillowcase or make sure your thread count is 700 or higher. Most wrinkles form during our sleep due to repetitive wrinkling from poor quality sheets and pillowcases. (I've heard that dermatologists can actually tell which side of the face a patient sleeps on just by the pattern of their wrinkles.)

Beauty tips and tricks

Eating right will go a long way toward making your skin look phenomenal, but there are also specific foods that boost your beauty. Raisins and prunes are great for dry skin and hair and weak nails. Every day, I drink an ounce of pomegranate concentrate—not a sweetened juice but a nutritious organic concentrate with resveratrol (made by AgroLabs and available at a handful of stores and online). One ounce a day does wonders. It's filled with powerful antioxidants that neutralize free radicals and support cardiovascular health. It's a wonder fruit. I highly recommend it for all those who want to look and feel better!

No matter how attractive you are, if you have bad posture, your entire image is ruined. To see if it needs improvement, stand against a wall with your heels touching the wall. If your heels, derriere, shoulder blades and the back of your head all touch the wall, you have the right posture. If there's a space between your head and the wall or your derriere and the wall, your posture needs work. This isn't just about how you look. Bodily posture affects your mind. Slumped shoulders and a bent spine can actually induce moodiness, and tensed stomach muscles also can induce anxiety.

I was on line at the grocery recently. In front of me was a mother with her teenage daughter. The daughter seemed very sad, and I noticed that her posture was very poor. One characteristic of people with low self-esteem is poor posture, so I decided to help this unhappy young woman. I struck up a conversation with her and told her that she had the most beautiful eyes I have ever seen, and that I wished I had eyes like her. I can't begin to explain the transition she made within a few short minutes. It was almost like a wilted flower being watered! She lit up and smiled and actually walked away with better posture! I felt a sense of elation myself, because self-esteem comes not only from being complimented, but also from creating goodness around you.

Did you wake up today with puffy eyes, or are you just plain bloated? Try jumping in place followed by some deep breathing. The body relies on external movement and breathing to keep fluids from pooling in areas such as eyes.

Be good to your skin. Never use water that's too hot or too cold to wash your face, as either one can cause broken capillaries and make your skin appear blotchy. I actually use pre-moistened wipes to wash my face, as they contain ingredients which are beneficial to skin without drying it out.

When applying moisturizer and/or sunscreen as part of your daily routine, don't neglect your hands! Hands are one of the biggest symbols of your age, so keep them moisturized and protected just as you would your face, neck and chest!

Part of good beauty is paying attention to the little details, such as your nails. It's more elegant to have short nails all the same length than uneven longer nails. Also, if your nails are bitten down to the skin, you're projecting an image of being nervous. Ladies, if your polish is chipped, remove it and start again!

Take the same care with your teeth. Brush two or three times a day, and floss at least once a day. Flossing daily, along with regular professional cleanings, helps prevent gum disease.

Gum disease and the inflammation it causes have now been linked to many systemic diseases, including heart disease, atherosclerosis, high cholesterol, Alzheimer's disease, type 2 diabetes, stroke, rheumatoid arthritis, chronic obstructive pulmonary disease (COPD) and pneumonia. Studies show that severe gum disease correlates with a dramatic increase in breast cancer.

Without regular flossing, your mouth and body can really suffer. Bacterial film (plaque) accumulates on neglected teeth below the gum line. Gums become irritated and bleed and your breath starts to smell bad. After a day or two plaque hardens into deposits—called tartar— that make it easier for more plaque to build up. Eventually, lack of flossing can lead to gingivitis, periodontal disease, and tooth loss. Fewer teeth lead to facial wrinkles and an aged appearance.

New research suggests that regular flossing may affect more than the health of your mouth. Flossing may protect your heart. Research has shown that periodontitis creates twice the risk of cardiovascular disease and elevated cholesterol. Flossing may protect your arteries. Researchers think that bacteria from the mouth may enter the bloodstream and contribute to inflammation and artery clogging. Flossing may reduce your risk of diabetes and its complications. Periodontal disease appears to make insulin resistance worse.

Oral care is about more than getting a clean bill of health at the dentist's office; it also results in a nicer smile and fresher breath.

SUE SAYS

It doesn't matter how good-looking you are—if your shoulders are slumped, you look insecure and unhappy. Stand up straight, hold your head up high, and show the whole world your "can do" attitude.

Make your own deep-cleansing fruit mask
With all-natural ingredients, this mask won't harm the skin and it works wonderfully! Here's what you'll need:

8 ounces plain yogurt
1 carrot
half a peach
half a cucumber

Chop the carrot, peach and cucumber into small pieces. Place all ingredients in a blender and blend until mixture becomes pasty. Apply to face and neck and let it sit for 10 minutes. Rinse off. Carrots are excellent anti-inflammatory agents, cucumbers help refresh and moisturize, and peaches have a super soothing effect. Your skin will be left soft, smooth and cleansed!

Stay in the shade
Limit your sun exposure. You need the vitamin D, but not the skin damage! Don't sit out in full sunlight all day, even with sunscreen. It may be tempting if you want that tan but we all know it's terrible for your skin. It ages you prematurely. And who wants to look red and sweaty all day? Be sensible: Stay in the shade during the hottest parts of the day.

Believe it or not, you can receive sun exposure even through your clothing. If you can see light through a fabric, damaging UV rays can get through as well. Try sun-blocking apparel if you're often outdoors in the sun. If being stylish is a priority, cover your face with a great hat and your legs with a beautiful maxi dress.

If it's already too late and you have a sunburn, here's a secret all the way from Russia: sour cream. Cold sour cream will help soothe irritated, sunburned skin while giving it a beautiful, bright glow. It works and it's cheap.

For all you guys who want to maintain a sexy stubble look all week long, use an electric beard trimmer on the lowest setting. This will keep the stubble from growing into a beard.

We all like to have a signature scent, so don't use scented deodorant, moisturizer and shampoo/conditioner at the same time, and then top it off with your favorite cologne or perfume. You'll just end up with a blurry line. Mix some unscented options into your routine to even things out. (Or, if you have a favorite perfume or cologne, you can see if it's offered as a powder or moisturizer and use that to layer a long-lasting scent. Just go light on each layer, or you'll risk having too strong a signature!)

Did you know that a visit to your dentist might just result in the face-lift you thought you needed? According to Dr. Robert Korwin, sagging cheeks and furrows are often caused by receding gums or bone, or teeth that become more crowded as we age. Changes inside your mouth provided by veneers, clear orthodontic aligners and other cosmetic dental devices may have a positive impact on your face as well as your smile! (Learn more at his website, www.drkorwin.com!)

I don't know about you, but it seems that as soon as I find a product I love, the company decides to discontinue it. Besides searching eBay, I found a great site for getting my lost favorites (for a while, anyway): www.discontinuedbeauty.com/store/.

Eat healthily. Move your body. Drink plenty of water. Get your beauty sleep. Repeat!

Accept or even trademark your beauty "flaws"

Most of us have some physical feature that we don't particularly like and sometimes wish we could change. If only my hair were straight. . . If only I could get rid of those dark circles under my eyes that everyone in my family has . . . If only I didn't have these freckles . . . If only my nose were smaller . . . then I would look better.

Do you pick yourself apart when you see yourself in a photo or video? Do you look in the mirror and only see what's imperfect about yourself? Make the continual effort on your part to learn to love the person you are, inside and out, every single day. Enhance and embrace the person you see in the mirror. Put up a sticky note that says, "I am gorgeous" and soon you'll start believing it!

Truth is, you were born with your face and the pieces belong together. You don't need to fit into some vague ideal of beauty. We aren't made by machines from a mold. Our differences are part of what makes us special. Be exactly who you are. Celebrate yourself!

There are things you may hate about yourself that others may find memorable. For instance, I always hated my curly hair as a kid. I only wanted the long, straight hair that most of my friends had. I used to straighten it, iron it, roll it on a beer can—I would stop at nothing to get it straight like everyone else.

Finally, I decided that I would just be myself. Now, my curly red hair is my trademark! It took an entire childhood of yearning for the silken straight locks of all my friends to reach this point. I only wish I'd known enough to appreciate what I had then. Today, all I want is more humidity to make it frizzier and curlier!

What about you? Could the "flaw" that bugs you so much turn out to be your trademark, one of the many things you are fondly known for?

If your "flaw" makes you feel anything but beautiful, consider this:

At the grocery store, you'll find people picking through stacked displays of perfectly uniform apples, pears, oranges and tomatoes. As we shop, we pick up each piece and look it over for any signs of inadequacy: a freckle, a bruise, a gouge or inconsistency in color. If we find anything, chances are we'll cast that piece aside and look for a better piece. And if we think the fruit is past its prime, we ditch it without a second thought.

What we don't consider is that, most of the time, appearance doesn't matter. The nutrients are still there, even if the carrot has a gnarly tip or the grapefruit isn't perfectly round. A lot of money is wasted in the agricultural industry because of this.

Use this as a metaphor for life: Beauty on the outside is just the rind. What's important is the nourishment that comes from within. Or, as the saying goes, "Like a pencil, the most important part of you will always be what's on the inside!"

Developing inner beauty is just as important as outer beauty. If you cannot make peace with your outer beauty, build your character through integrity and you will be beautiful on the inside as well as the outside. To me, the most important qualities in a person are character and integrity. I meet so many attractive people who seem wonderful, but then I realize after a time that they have no character. It's just a façade. The apple may look red and shiny on the outside, but you can still bite into it and find a worm!

I don't care how much money you have or how many celebrities you may know, it's what's inside you that really counts. At the end of the day, those with character and integrity are the people I want to spend my time with.

Have you ever looked into a magnifying mirror and been horrified at the sight? We notice every single pore, every blemish, every flaw possible. Our logic fails us, we concentrate on one detail of our face that we hate, and we ultimately disregard the big picture. Well, if you think about it, who really sees you that way except you? In life, we all tend to magnify our faults, enlarging every perceived flaw until our self-esteem plummets. Today, let's start magnifying our achievements and minimizing our faults. Look into that mirror and see you for who you really are: Amazing!

Whatever you do, don't try to hide your perceived imperfections from the world. None of us is perfect. Trying to be something you are not will always come across to people. Relax, laugh at yourself, and you will be surprised at how people will be more attracted to you.

SUE SAYS
You can't find real peace and happiness when you don't know who you really are. For better or worse, accept yourself, accept your flaws and your talents. The result: You won't need constant validation because you know who is staring back at you in the mirror!

About cellulite
Cellulite is a common beauty "flaw" for women. Basically, it's a combination of fat, water and wastes trapped beneath the skin. It's not about being fat; cellulite can be seen on otherwise thin women. When circulation is impaired, fat gets trapped in pockets just beneath the skin instead of being expelled by normal means. Over time, it hardens and forms that puckering skin effect. Because it is unattached material, dieting and exercising alone can't dislodge cellulite. Most people who have cellulite have it because of genetics, but it also results from poor nutrition. Inadequate exercise and insufficient water intake increase the trapped wastes and toxins. And crash dieting with rapid regain of weight increases cellulite formation.

So, what can you do about it? I found these tips in a book called *Healthy Healing* by Dr. Linda Page:

Eliminate all fried and fatty dairy foods from your diet; also, red meat and extra salty foods.

Yoga and Pilates promote deep breathing, which moves out lymph congestion that shows as cellulite. Body Innovations Cellulite Eraser Body Spray firms the skin, reducing the look of cellulite for five hours.

Making peace with aging

Okay, I admit it. I have found this aging process stuff a bit difficult to handle. In the last year, some things have exacerbated this feeling: a photo taken of me in which I saw a middle-aged woman (Who is this? When did this happen?), and the constant onslaught of Facebook photos from elementary, junior high and high school in which I am tagged. Looking at these photos reminds me of time gone by . . . and how I'm now at the place in my life where my mom was when I thought she was "old."

Fear of aging is a common thread for all of us over 40s (that's all I will say). It's a difficult process to wrap our minds around. I spent many years working in the fashion and beauty industries, where youth and looks are honored. The catwalks are filled with young models without a line on their faces. The media cherishes young, up-and-coming actors and singers; everyone wants to know what they're wearing. The rare times we see an older celebrity, it's either to admonish his potbelly or her sagging face, or to celebrate those over 40 who "don't look their age." (I believe they don't look their age because they've been surgically enhanced. And that's what's celebrated!)

Aging represents many things: Will I become invisible? Will I lose my beauty, my memory, respect? Let's face it. We're all aging. It's a natural process everyone goes through, but we still want to stay young for as long as we can. Many of us (I know I do) work hard to defy the odds of aging by eating right, exercising daily and slathering on moisturizer day and night. The cosmetics, fashion, skincare and hair care industries are cashing in on age-defying products, which are top sellers in all categories. Plastic surgery is extremely popular for those who seek more extreme measures to look younger.

I used to watch in awe as my grandparents, with their gray hair and wrinkles, would exude peace and contentment. They couldn't do all the things they did when they were young, yet they were happy. They knew that they earned every wrinkle by raising eight children and running a successful business, which was handed down to their sons. They had many hobbies and talents, which kept them busy and satisfied, and their many grandchildren filled their hearts with joy.

My generation will live longer than the generations before us. Fifty is today what 40 was a generation ago. This is great news. But the fact that we're living longer makes it even more necessary for us to embrace and learn to accept the aging process. We cannot control it, so we might as well control our reaction to it.

Sad to say, many people let themselves go because they feel like they don't matter any more after a certain age. There is a choice. I'm not in my twenties anymore, but I take much better care of myself now than I did back then. Of course, certain things can't be avoided. No matter how much cream I apply, my skin won't be the same as when I was 20. But without exercising and eating right, I imagine I'd look a lot older than I do. The aging process can be improved if you are willing to put in the effort to do so.

The direction each of us chooses to take will determine whether we enjoy or dread the rest of our lives. We can remain fearful of aging and stay stuck in the past, or we can accept this natural cycle of life and look for new opportunities. It is never too late to look inward at who you really are and not allow society to dictate what your value is. Follow your passion, whether it is helping people, animals or the planet. Help is needed everywhere. Realize the importance of family and true friends, those who accept you for who you truly are. If we keep all the focus on aging, we are not living!

I'm gradually reaching a place of peace within myself where the inevitability of aging loses its power to overwhelm me. I can't run away from or ignore the fact that I don't own the same face I had when I was younger. But I can revel in the fact that I've earned every year I've been alive and am grateful for each one.

If we start each day with the philosophy that life is only beginning, we will stay young and vital until we take our last breath. Sometimes, when I lament my age and wish I could be younger, I stop myself and realize that it is my spirit of adventure and zest for life that has me looking forward to each new day. Try to keep your soul youthful right up to old age and celebrate the days ahead instead of mourning the days gone by. Inner happiness will ensue with this mindset.

I am all for looking your best at every age. We should do all we can to eat right, exercise and live as stress-free as possible. Many people resort to plastic surgery, Botox and other superficial methods as the way to feel better about themselves. If you're not fixed from the inside, no amount of scrubs, peels, or facial alterations will fill the void that lies deep within. Remember, a nail in a piece of wood will not hold a house together if the foundation is cracked. Learn to love and fix what's inside first.

What makes anyone attractive is not always just a good looking face or fit body. We are all more than the sum of our parts. What's on the inside can make a huge difference in what we perceive as beauty on the outside. You can have the most beautiful face and yet be unattractive, or not have a perfect face, yet be irresistible. In order to have the purest beauty, you must be beautiful on the inside first. As this inner radiance shines through, those around you will find you far more attractive than skin deep alone.

SUE SAYS

Times change as do the seasons, but as long as we keep our-selves open to recognizing the beauty of each season, we can survive the seasons of life in peace.

Creating Your Personal Style

Beauty is ten, nine of which is dressing.

—Azerbaijani proverb

Fashion and style are not frivolous topics. They're a very serious part of our civilization, something in which every person participates, whether he or she likes it or not. We all have to get dressed in the morning. And what you look like is your statement to the public.

Image counts! How we dress has a huge impact on the people we meet professionally and socially. It affects how they view and treat us. Someone who isn't quite sure how to pull it all together may be seen as lacking self-esteem, while a well-dressed individual is usually seen as self-confident, giving him or her a clear advantage. It takes only four seconds for someone to form an impression of you. Keep in mind the second golden rule: "You never get a second chance to make a first impression."

Once, I attended a designer show house in New York City that con-sisted of two apartments, each with five rooms. The first was decorated in a flamboyant way, lots of color and eccentricity. The second was subdued, in muted colors, with floral arrangements. I loved them both, even though their styles were completely different. It reminded me: You don't have to look like everyone else in order to be attractive. Just make sure you have a defined personal style.

So what's your personal style? Even if you don't think much about how you dress now, you can still learn to develop your own unique style. And you might find that you enjoy getting dressed when the end result truly reflects and enhances you—when it says something true about your personality, and brings out your best features for everyone to see!

The simple secret to a successful appearance is to be the best version of yourself, not a copy of someone else, be they a friend, acquaintance or TV celebrity. Why would a Chihuahua try to look like a greyhound, or vice versa? Be your authentic self and your true greatness will appear.

What is personal style?

Fashions fade, style is eternal.
—Yves Saint Laurent

Isn't it interesting that Yves Saint Laurent, one of the style icons of our generation, designer of apparel, accessories and more, would admit that the clothes we wear aren't the only thing that defines who we are!

Having style is more than just wearing designer couture and following the latest celebrity trend. To have a great individual style, one must be creative and innovative. Think of Fashion as the artist's palette and Style as the finished portrait. Style is your personal expression. It's what makes you stand out from the crowd.

I'm sure you have seen those people who just have a flair about them. That's what I mean by personal style. Like the gentleman who knows exactly how to wear the sports jacket with the pocket square and the right sunglasses to effect a great look. Or the woman whose dress, handbag and heels don't match color-wise but look so chic when put together. I know someone who only wears plaids; that may not be your taste, but it certainly sets this person apart!

I inherited a love of fashion from my mom, although our tastes are vastly different. She put together outfits in ways that attracted compliments. For instance, she would use the fabric that was shed from her altered clothing and apply it to shoes so that her shoes matched her dress or slacks. No one else would even think of that! Also, she always wore a stylish hat and sunglasses. This sense of style was just something she had within her, maybe because she was an artist. Style is something unique to you, and only you.

Style has been defined by fashion gurus as "a distinctive way of doing something, a fashionable way of living, graceful manners and distinctive appearance." The word I want to focus on here is distinctive. True style is not about being a carbon copy of what you see in the magazines. It's about expressing your individuality in the clothes you wear. If you love what you wear, people will see it through your clothes.

A perennially stylish person keeps up with trends but doesn't follow them blindly. Someone who dresses only in the latest trends is as much a fashion victim as someone who pays absolutely no attention to how he or she dresses. The more you learn about fashion and develop and refine your own style, the more comfortable you'll become with breaking the rules—and being smart about which fashion risks to take.

How to develop your own personal style
How can you develop your personal sense of style? Basically, it's about setting yourself apart from the crowd in even a small way. With all the generic mall stores, fashion can start to look homogenized—you can't tell J. Crew from The Gap. But we aren't interchangeable, and we shouldn't dress as if we stepped off an assembly line. Don't be afraid to try out many different styles!

Look to people who you think have great style. Don't copy exactly what they do but start to notice what they do to set themselves apart. Maybe she picks a studded belt to go with her plain black dress, or he opts for argyle socks instead of basic black with his slacks. This is style. Think outside the box.

Experiment with colors, textures, patterns and layering. Try changing up your look by visiting a local vintage shop or a unique boutique you've never tried before. An easy way to start is with items close to home. For instance, try stealing something from your boyfriend's or husband's closet. How about taking a cardigan of his, wearing it over leggings and belting it?

Know yourself when it comes to accessories. What do you always reach for in your own closet? Are you always throwing on a scarf (even in the summer) or wearing a favorite piece of turquoise jewelry? Do you prefer cowboy boots or like the attention you get when you wear a particular pair of funky glasses? If there's something you love to wear, get more of it and make it your trademark. Celebrate the things that make you happy!

Is there a celebrity—present-day or past—who you think has an interesting sense of style? Use what he or she wears to broaden your fashion education. Pay attention to the things you like about their style and start incorporating those details into your own closet. Having your own style icons can help you determine what you like and what you might want to try. Use them as a springboard to discover new things!

Also, keep in mind that you don't have to accept clothes and accessories precisely as you purchase them. Being original is about being creative if you see a different use. For example, I get many compliments about a particular dress I wear that was not meant to be a dress! It's actually the under-layer of a crocheted sweater dress by Legatte, one of my favorite designers. When I bought the sweater dress, I noticed the gold slip underneath it and decided to wear it alone. I added a belt, and voilà! It looks great and attracts attention. If you see something you really like, keep an open mind about how you might use it!

Developing personal style is about being authentic—true to you. It's not about pleasing others. If you're dressing for others' approval, what you wear is more a costume than a true reflection of you.

If you have an individual sense of style or something about you isn't mainstream, be proud! Don't try to be a cardboard cutout of someone else's style or personality. There are always going to be people who scoff and gossip within earshot, but as long as you say to yourself "This is just the way I am," you'll have more self-respect than if you cave in and conform.

Having style is about setting yourself apart. Be unique. Be an individual. If you are different, be proud. Being different is beautiful and it attracts the right people into your life!

SUE SAYS
You don't have to be a superstar. Just get out there and be the best person you can be! Even small deeds are purposeful!

Comfortable or stylish?
Which one are you? Would you rather sacrifice some comfort to look good, or always be comfortable, even if it means wearing clothes or shoes that aren't in style?

I think it's possible to be both. You simply have to be creative. There are chic outfits made of fabrics as soft and forgiving as they are beautiful.

And trends, with a little effort, can always be translated into more comfortable expressions.

I know a woman who says that, because her feet have no arches to speak of, her stilettos actually feel good on! However, if you're not into sky-high heels, try kitten heels or resolve to have the world's greatest collection of funky, stylish flats. The more things you try on, the more likely you will be to find good-looking pieces that feel good, too.

If you really want both comfort and style, go for it!

Dress to feel better

I very often have folks ask me where I'm going because I seem dressed up to them (this usually happens at the grocery store). Since when is anyone not wearing sweatpants and a hoodie breaking the rules? I don't believe that dressing up should be reserved for special occasions. Why waste an outfit you spent a fortune on by wearing it once?

The next time you feel the urge to throw on a baggy t-shirt and worn-out pants to go out, take some advice from fashion expert Jacqui Ripley: "Anything that makes you feel frumpy, dumpy and lumpy does nothing for your sense of self."

It's true. Even if you think it doesn't matter, even if you think you won't be seen, try dressing up the next time you go to the store. See how it makes you feel.

If you work at home, are a stay-at-home mom or aren't working, make an effort to dress every day as if you are going out. This will change your whole approach to even the most boring household chores.

Don't overdo it, but do take risks with your style. It's always better to be a little overdressed than underdressed in a situation. Think about where you are going, and kick it up a notch!

Sometimes our problem of being in a rut is staring right at us. The way you look on the outside directly affects how you feel on the inside. Simple things such as proper posture, good dental health, a nice hairstyle and a new outfit can help you feel better. Looking good on the outside will make you feel a little better on the inside, and that is the perfect start to a new you!

Stop caring about what people think of you. It really doesn't matter. If you're focused on whether people think you are good-looking, funny, fat or skinny, it's impossible to be yourself. If you change to fit into one group, you'll have to continue changing to fit into other groups down the road. It will never end. Rather than trying to be someone you are not, be the best version of yourself.

Style on a budget

Fashion can be bought, style one must possess.
—Edna Woolman Chase

Having style doesn't require having lots of money. Once you understand your personal style, you'll find it easier to locate and acquire new pieces from a variety of places, not just the most expensive boutiques.

One day a friend was wearing a gorgeous Prada clutch along with a very stylish pair of Tod's loafers. After complimenting her on her good taste (and, I must admit, being a little mystified about how she afforded these purchases), she told me both items were purchased from her favorite consignment shop near her home on the Upper East Side of Manhattan.

With the economy sagging, many people are giving up their designer clothing and accessories to consignment shops in order to recoup some money from their investment.

At my friend's favorite shop, the affluent ladies (and men) who tire of their gently worn apparel, jewelry, shoes, etc., consign their pieces with the most potential. It's a great way to earn back some of their money spent on luxury items that are not being used.

Usually women and men who sell to high-end consignment shops buy their items from a wide array of places, Europe and Asia included. A lot of pieces are unique, and not something you'll find everywhere. If you are looking to pump up your wardrobe with designer clothes, this is a great, cost-effective way to do it. You might even find items that have been on your wish list for a while!

Since she told me about her favorite shop, my friend never ceases to amaze me with the items she finds. I myself have brought some of my "worn twice" outfits and coats to this shop and made something from the transaction. It may not be what I put into it, but at least I got something back. I also came out of one transaction with a gorgeous pair of Cavalli sunglasses that cost me 70 percent less than retail!

When you're consignment shopping, remember that the best consignment stores are usually in affluent, fashion-forward neighborhoods. Expect to save about 70 percent off the retail price. The best time to buy current merchandise is halfway through a season; usually fashionistas are already tired of their outfits and accessories by then. Shop by your senses. Feel the fabric, make sure it feels right.

Don't necessarily buy something at the consignment shop just because it's a great deal. Buy it because you love it and will wear it. Even if you find a Versace dress at an amazing price, if you know it's not for you, don't waste your money. Don't ever buy anything without trying it on. Many items in high-end shops are European, and the sizes may be completely different than what you're used to.

Bottom line, if you've been drooling over that "it" bag or a Chanel bouclé jacket, try your hand at consignment. You might be pleasantly surprised at how much (especially in this economy) you'll find. Maybe you can acquire those Louboutins you've been dreaming of . . . .and who will ever know?

Never underestimate the power of details

A well-tied tie is the first serious step in life.

—Oscar Wilde

It may sound crazy, but Oscar Wilde designed his wife's clothes and gave lectures on aesthetics. He knew that how we dress transmits powerful signals and that attention to detail makes a huge difference.

As your sense of personal style develops, you'll start to notice details big and small. Keep refining them. And if you really want to make a difference in your wardrobe in a hurry, consult a friend with a good eye or a stylist (like me).

Start with the basics. Aim to be well-groomed and well put together every day. In general, always wear nice clothes. As Coco Chanel told us, you never know when you will have a date with destiny, so be sure to be dressed for it. Remember that a great smile and self-confidence are two accessories that go with every outfit. (You wear the most expensive clothes, but if you slouch and look at the floor, you'll look terrible no matter what you're wearing.)

Dress for your body type. We all have little flaws, no matter what shape we're in. These flaws can be accentuated when we wear clothing that does not suit our body type. Wearing the right clothes can go a long way toward making your flaws evaporate! For instance, if your legs are longer than your body, create a balance by wearing jeans or skirts that fit at the hips instead of the waist. If you're a guy and can't get that V shape in your torso from working out, a double-breasted jacket with padded shoulders will accentuate your chest and shoulders. For ladies seeking longer looking legs, always wear a high heel. Cinching a wide belt around the smallest part of your torso—your natural waist—emphasizes and slims this zone while accentuating your sexy curves.

Most people would like to look taller and thinner than they are. Your clothing can do a lot to make you seem that way. Wear one solid color (preferably dark) from head to toe, to make the body look fluid rather than cutting it off in the middle. Vertical stripes tend to act like an optical illusion, making your entire torso appear longer. Always wear at least a one-inch heel. And did you know that wearing shoes with pointed toes will make you look slimmer? If you are wearing slacks, shoes with pointed toes allow the length to flow to a point, as opposed to rounded-toe shoes which cut off the line and make your legs look more stumpy. Always wear the same color hose as skirt, to lengthen the line. Avoid anything pleated!

Wear clothes that fit. Your clothes should touch your body without being too tight. Clothes that are too loose can kill a fabulous figure, and can make a larger-than-average person look bigger than she or he actually is.

Don't be afraid of color, ladies and gentlemen. It attracts compliments!

Invest in accessories, whether scarves, jewelry, pins, pocket squares, ties, shoes or hats. They can change your look from ordinary to extraordinary. Usually the last thing on is the first thing noticed, such as a great belt on a woman or, for men, a subtle pocket square or the way he knots his tie. Choose silver accessories if your skin color is cool and gold if your skin color is warm. (I also like silver more for men!) Combining great accessories with your basic wardrobe will make you look coordinated and chic!

Ladies, rethink how you wear a suit. I believe that looking sexy in a suit is as simple as skipping the blouse and either wearing a camisole or bustier, or if the suit's not too low cut, skip anything underneath. A belt at the waist and a pair of stilettos will finish off the look.

Men, invest in jeans that fit really well (meaning, not baggy in the butt). They should hug the butt, but not too tightly. Have two styles in your wardrobe: a lighter pair to wear casually with a nice sweater or shirt, and a darker, more fitted straight leg pair to wear with a blazer (a men's must!) for a more formal, polished look that will work almost anywhere.

And ladies and men, trade any baggy tees and sweatpants for workout apparel that's more stylish. Target and many other stores carry great contemporary workout gear at reasonable prices.

Details for men

Let's be honest. Most of you men out there, until early adulthood, were likely taught not to place too much importance on what you wear. Now that you actually do care (or so I hope), you need to learn or put into practice a few basics to keep you well-dressed for now and for the rest of your life. I have a few tricks for you to keep in mind.

Even if you spend a fortune on the latest designer wear, little blunders can ruin your entire look. Don't feel bad—many of these mistakes are common. If you're guilty of any of these, you are not alone!

Many men forget to put on a belt. This is fine if you're going for a casual look, with your shirt over your pants. (Just make sure your pants aren't falling down.) However, if your shirt is tucked into your pants, a belt is mandatory. It ties your whole outfit together. When dressed for a special occasion, an elegant belt is like your jewelry.

The kind of belt can vary. As long as it fits properly in the loops, it doesn't matter if it's wide or narrow. The important thing is that a belt can be an amazing fashion accessory. Choose a classy buckle (Ferragamo makes nice ones) to make your ensemble *très magnifique!*

Pant length is important. Different pant styles look best at different lengths. Jeans, for example, can extend all the way to the bottom of your shoe; you'll actually look longer and leaner by wearing them this way. However, dress pants should end at the top of your heel—but be careful that your socks don't show when you walk and that no more than two inches of your socks are visible when you're sitting. Unless you're walking in a flood, avoid cuffing up your jeans and pants.

Chunky shoes paired with slim-fitting pants is a serious fashion faux pas. If the bottom of the pants is very narrow, you'll end up looking like a clown. Many commercial shoe stores carry lots of thick-soled shoes, but I suggest you choose classic slim shoes, loafers or European-style dress shoes with your pants. The chunky-shoe look is not quite as terrible with jeans; just make sure the bottom of the jean leg is not narrow (you want a boot cut style).

Don't wear scuffed shoes, ever! It takes away from an otherwise nice ensemble.

Never wear white socks with dark pants or jeans. You don't want people staring at your ankles! Always match your socks to your slacks. For

Lessons from Life Coaching • 163

example, if you are wearing a navy suit and brown shoes, I recommend dark blue socks. You can also wear neutral brown socks to blend with the shoes. Stick to blacks, grays, browns and dark blues.

Avoid novelty clothing. Even if you are a huge fan of Star Wars, you don't have to advertise it to the world. Same goes for blinking ties. If you want to look like you have class and sophistication, stay away from these!

Always avoid short-sleeved shirts paired with a tie. For that matter, I don't care for short-sleeved dress shirts at all. To me, they look silly. A long-sleeved button-down shirt is much more appealing, with a tie or on its own!

Go for good proportion. Don't wear baggy pants with an equally baggy shirt. It will make you look fat. On the other side of the coin, a tight shirt with equally tight pants will make you look like John Travolta in *Saturday Night Fever*. Balance is best.

Don't wear too much jewelry. A nice watch is sufficient, but avoid bling. Too many rings, necklaces, etc. just takes away from a sophisticated look.

Invest in a good manicure set. Don't show off bitten fingernails. People will wonder what you're so nervous about!

In reality, the way you dress is the first thing people notice. And the first impression you make can be critical to your success. Avoiding these common fashion blunders will help you down the right path to looking very well put together!

Upgrade your image—affordably!
If you're feeling down about yourself right now, here's some good advice: change your image! Once you get your outside reflecting all the good stuff you have on the inside, you'll be amazed at how many other things fall into place—higher-self esteem, better job opportunities and perhaps even that special relationship. And it doesn't have to cost a lot if you follow my budget-friendly image tips.

Organize your closet, clearing out things you haven't worn in the past year. Donate them to a local charity or bring them to a consignment shop. Make room for a few updated outfits. Having a neat, clean space makes it easier to choose the right outfit every day.

Get proper undergarments that fit correctly. Visible panty lines are a no-no, as is an ill-fitting bra. Your local department store or specialty shop has experts on hand to help you choose something flattering.

Always practice good posture. This is one of the strongest points I stress to people. If you slouch, you're telling the world that you have no self-confidence. So, stand up straight, with your shoulders back. Walk tall with pride. After all, you are something special and everyone should know it!

Start an exercise regimen. It's one of the most important things we can do for ourselves! There are so many benefits to taking care of your body through exercise and proper diet. Not only will you look better in clothes, but you will also feel better overall, sleep better and have an extra spring in your step.

If you want to look younger longer, cut out smoking, excessive alcohol consumption and sunbathing! In the short term, these things make you look good, but in the long run, you'll age way before your time. All of these vices speed up the aging process.

If your hair and makeup are dating you, change your look! Go to a reputable hair salon for advice and look to a cosmetics counter or store for tips on makeup application.

Get a great bag. It can be a real fashion statement on its own. Look at a woman walking down the street wearing just sweats. If she's carrying a great bag, it automatically upgrades her image. This is true for men, too. Carrying a messenger bag or attaché that is ragged and disheveled will ruin an otherwise polished look.

Upgrade your image, and you'll be amazed at how quickly all your other goals fall in line. Packaging yourself will attract people and opportunities like nothing else will!

What to wear in the workplace

The business world today is like a chess game. Wearing the right clothes is a basic strategy in order to win. Just as an Olympic skier uses the best equipment to gain a competitive edge, dressing with style and panache gives you a jump start in climbing the ladder of success.

Think of it like this: You're a walking billboard for your company or place of business. Do you want people to drive by the billboard and pay it no mind, or do you want them to be attracted to that billboard and call the next day for your business? If you are self-employed, the rules are the same. You are the commercial for yourself.

In a matter of just seconds, we decide how to respond to someone based on what we see. Grooming, attire and posture are the first three things we notice. It seems unfair, but we often associate well-dressed individuals with intelligence and high achievement. That's why they usually get more opportunities in the business world.

Dress like you are worth the money you want to earn. Anything does not go as far as I'm concerned. Being sloppy and not "put together" will leave you at the bottom of the food chain when it comes to promotions and opportunities. Invest in well-made, tailored outfits. They don't have to be super-expensive, just very well made.

Avoid looking sloppy. No wrinkled clothing. No baggy clothing. And, depending on where you work, women should avoid clothing that is too revealing (see-through blouses and skirts that are too short, for example). You may get attention, but that kind of attention has its pitfalls.

Traditional business attire is still alive and well, and business casual is also very popular right now. For men who want to appear more casual, don't do jeans and t-shirts. Make sure you're still wearing quality button-down shirts with dressy trousers. Pair these with stylish leather shoes that are always polished and kept in good condition. Keep your belt the same color as your shoes.

It's funny, but color plays a big part in a professional image. Red usually implies an aggressive person; navy, trustworthy; gray, conservative; and black, chic.

Remember, in a business setting, you are how you appear. Image is directly linked to success potential. You want to command respect and trust. Your attire has its own language, and it can say that you're a leader with potential or yell out that you're a loser.

How to dress for an interview

What we wear to a job interview is a clue about ourselves that we want the world to discover. The more polished and professional we appear, the sooner we'll be on our way to new career opportunities. Investing in the right power outfit is an investment in your future.

The business climate is only becoming more competitive and demanding, so standing out is very important. You want your first impression to be great, not just good. Easily half of how you are perceived is how you look. This is what the employer first notices about you.

A man who wears a suit and tie to an interview will make a much better impression than one who is wearing jeans and a t-shirt, even if the job environment is casual. A dark suit with coordinated shirt and tie, dark socks and dark leather shoes are a good investment outfit for interviews. Hair should be neat. Never pile on the cologne! Bitten nails are a no-no, so make sure they are trimmed neatly before the interview. Carrying an organizer or a briefcase rounds out the package.

A woman who walks into an interview wearing a too-short skirt or too-low-cut blouse will probably not get the job (unless it's for Hooters). Instead, she should wear a simple dress or suit that ends just below the knees. Her shoes should be conservative; heels are okay but nothing too chunky. Pantyhose should be a neutral color; no fishnet stockings. Keep the perfume light and make sure nails are neatly manicured.

Other things potential employers will notice (and not take kindly to): Chewing gum. Answering your cell phone in the middle of the interview. Carrying your iPod. Carrying bottled water or drinks of any kind. Bringing in food items. Remember, you're there for the interview and nothing else!

Swimsuits: how to look good with your body shape

A survey done in 2007 among nearly 2,000 women uncovered that 90 percent of them were concerned about their appearance in a swimsuit. No surprise! Most women dread shopping for one. There's not much to hide when we put on a swimsuit; no wonder it makes us nervous! But, if you know your body type and what works for you, then you might actually come to enjoy it!

Whether you have a big stomach, wide hips, fat thighs or too large breasts, I promise there's a swimsuit out there for you! Some people have more than one problem area, so be innovative and take hints from all solutions. The right swimsuit can take pounds off your body. The wrong style can do the opposite, making you even more self-conscious and bringing attention to the areas you want to hide.

Think of three words: color, construction, cut.

If you have a big stomach, go for colors that are dark. If the suit is two-toned, go for a darker color on the bottom, lighter on the top. Bold prints can distract the eye away from the stomach. Don't wear horizontal stripes, only vertical. Ruched fabrics and textured surfaces hold you in and look great with a sarong, which also takes the focus away from the tummy. Definitely stick with a one-piece suit or wear a tankini.

If you think you have a large backside, dark colors are the way to go, as are large prints. Go for a high-cut leg rather than a bottom half that sits low on your behind. Avoid boy shorts; they'll only make your backside appear bigger.

If you have large hips, bring attention to the top part of your body for balance. Halter tops and bikinis that have a print on top and plain bottoms work well. Avoid high cut styles, as they emphasize the hips.

If you have super broad shoulders and slim hips and thighs, a cute string bikini would look great on you.

If you have a big bust, go for a style with a deep vee or plunge neck. It will elongate your figure and lessen the fullness of your breast area, while still allowing you to show off your cleavage. Avoid spaghetti straps and bandeau-style swimsuits that don't have a tie at the neck. These will only make you look more top-heavy. Underwire cups will also give you support and lift.

If you have a small bust, your best bet is European designers, as they tend to design for women with small tops. A good choice is a push-up style bra which will give you more cleavage. A bandeau-style top would also look great on you!

One of the recent trends for swimwear is the one-shoulder, asymmetrical style. It can work for you or against you, depending on your body type. One-shouldered suits can accentuate the bust line, while vertical asymmetric lines can minimize it, along with slimming a large tummy.

As a rule, a one-piece suit is more flattering than a bikini on most women. But be careful with the cutaway style. This style suits only those with toned bodies.

If you're not planning on swimming, don't be afraid to wear a cool necklace. A necklace is a great way to draw attention away from your bottom half if that's where you're heavy.

Don't wear big, baggy cover-ups if you can help it. They will only make you look bigger. Maxi dresses are always in style, so try wearing one over your suit. You can find them everywhere, in every price range.

You can also look stylish by wearing great strappy sandals instead of Crocs or sneakers. After all the effort you have put into looking great in your swimsuit, why ruin it with the wrong pair of shoes! A great pair of sunglasses and a wide-brimmed hat will not only keep your skin looking great, but will help you to finish off your look.

Glasses as a fashion accessory

Start thinking of glasses as an important fashion statement, not just a functional item. They announce much about who you are. Wearing the correct style can create an immediate positive impression about you, especially if it's the first.

If you are wearing frames that are ten years old, they may serve their basic purpose, but they are probably aging you. Nothing dates a person more than the eyeglasses they're wearing. If you see someone wearing rimless glasses or half glasses, they are automatically labeled as older. Or, on the other hand, think of the TV series "Ugly Betty." Those thick lenses are used to make Betty appear nerdy and unattractive. Think about how just changing the glasses would change her look.

It's interesting how sculpted metal or plastic can define your style to others. Glasses can make you look trendy and edgy, artsy, intellectual, authoritative and even sexy. Many times I will point out a man or woman because of the glasses they are wearing. They are a reflection of your style sense and can make or break your look. If you haven't had your vision checked in a while, this might be a good opportunity to change your look. You may even look five years younger!

Nearly every house of fashion has its logo on a line of sunglasses, and just like clothing, they launch new lines seasonally. Every spring and fall, there are new styles, trends, shapes, colors and technology. If you want to look better and more up to date, invest in new, stylish glasses.

Here are some basic principles to consider when picking out your perfect frame:

If you're over 40, pick a frame that will make you look younger, for example, a frame that's horizontal with a slight upward tilt at the edges. Avoid frames that slope downward. Upturned frames draw the eye upward and accentuate your cheekbones. Frames that slope downward will make your face look droopy.

Choose a frame that brings warmth, color and softness to your face. The frame should complement your face shape, face size, eye color, hair color and skin tone. A perfect frame will bring you to a new style level and bring out your best features. (If you are lucky to find a great optician, as I did, you'll have plenty of help making a good choice.)

If you're blond, white and translucent frames tend to look good, as do most medium-tone colors such as browns, tortoiseshells and yellow or rose undertones.

If you're a redhead, like me, go with warm browns and tortoiseshells to be safe, but don't be afraid to try burgundy. As a matter of fact, I have a pair of orange Chanels that look great on me. I love them!

If you have brown hair, a red frame would be striking.

If your hair is black, black frames always look good, but avoid extremely light-colored frames.

If you are gray-haired, choose a vibrant color to add some panache to your look. The only color that won't look good is tortoiseshell, which is too yellow-hued to be flattering.

The myth of age-appropriate dressing

Some women and men, when they reach a certain age (over 40), suddenly seem to adopt a dour, boring fashion sense. I have seen women, as soon as they reach 40, cut their hair, wear shapeless outfits (which de-feminize and de-sexualize them) and basically decide it's time to throw in the towel. Not true! There's no reason why women and men of a certain age aren't supposed to be sexy just because they're nestled in a marriage, working in the business world or caring for parents and grandchildren.

Simple, effortless, sophisticated style oozes sex appeal if you feel comfortable in your own skin. A pair of jeans with a pair of stilettos is sexy without looking like you're trying to compete with your daughters (or granddaughters). There's no reason, if you take care of yourself, to stop showing off your hard-earned figure, and you can do it in a more elegant way than a twenty-year-old. Make it work for you and people will always be saying "Who is she?" and not "Who is she kidding?"

Don't believe the myth that after a certain age you shouldn't draw attention to yourself. Just do it in a refined way!

Affirm yourself

Here is an affirmation to recite each and every day: "I am extremely beautiful/handsome. I don't care what other people think or say about me, because I know my self-worth."

Now, go live it.

About the Author

Susan Korwin is a Certified Life Coach who was trained through the prestigious Life Coach Institute. She is a contributing writer for *Total Prestige* magazine, *Latino Show* magazine and *Jersey Shore Woman* and has done fashion modeling for Dolita Paris collection and Diane King of Got Entertainment. Her popular Facebook page is visited by hundreds of fans every day (www.facebook.com/pages/Susan-Korwin-Life-and-Style-Consultant) and her website blog has dozens of helpful articles (www.susankorwin.com). Susan was recently named one of the "Top 20 Most Inspiring Individuals in New York City." While attending Hunter College majoring in Psychology, Susan worked in the fashion and media industry, including such prestigious companies as Bloomingdale's, Revlon, and Media Networks. Susan has three sons, Joshua, Zachary, and Devin, and lives in New Jersey with her husband, cosmetic and implant dentist, Robert Korwin, DMD MICOI MAGD.